5/17/91

LOVE
AND ITS PLACE
IN NATURE

LOVE AND ITS PLACE IN NATURE

A Philosophical Interpretation of Freudian Psychoanalysis

JONATHAN LEAR

Farrar, Straus & Giroux

NEW YORK

Library of Congress Cataloging-in-Publication Data
Lear, Jonathan.
Love and its place in nature : a philosophical interpretation
of Freudian psychoanalysis / Jonathan Lear. — 1st ed.
p.   cm.
Includes bibliographical references and index.
1. Love. 2. Psychoanalysis—Philosophy. I. Title.
BF175.5.L68L42   1990   150.19′52—dc20   90-33899 CIP

This book is dedicated to

FRANCES LEAR
and
NORMAN LEAR
and
HANS LOEWALD

who in their distinctive ways inspired it

CONTENTS

Perhaps this is the moment, my friends, to indulge on this festive occasion in a little polemic against Freud himself. He does not esteem philosophy very highly. His scientific exactitude does not permit him to regard it as a science. He reproaches it with imagining that it can present a continuous and consistent picture of the world; with overestimating the objective value of logical operations; with believing in intuitions as a source of knowledge and with indulging in positively animistic tendencies, in that it believes in the magic of words and the influence of thought upon reality. But would philosophy really be thinking too highly of itself on these assumptions? Has the world ever been changed by anything save by thought and its magic vehicle the Word? I believe that in actual fact philosophy ranks before and above the natural sciences and that all method and exactness serve its intuitions and its intellectual and historical will. In the last analysis it is always a matter of the *quod erat demonstrandum*. Scientific freedom from assumptions is or should be a moral fact. But intellectually it is, as Freud points out, probably an illusion. One might strain the point and say that science has never made a discovery without being authorized and encouraged thereto by philosophy.

All this is by the way . . .

THOMAS MANN, "Freud and the Future,"
read by Mann to Freud in Vienna on May 9, 1936,
the occasion of Freud's eightieth birthday

. . . we proceed to treat of living creatures, without omitting, to the best of our ability, any member of the kingdom, however ignoble. For if some have no graces to charm the sense, yet nature, which fashioned them, gives amazing pleasure in their study to all who can trace links of causation, and are inclined to philosophy. Indeed, it would be strange if representations of them were attractive, because they disclose the mimetic skill of the painter or sculptor, and the original realities themselves were not more interesting, to all at any rate who have eyes to discern causes. We therefore must not recoil with childish aversion from the examination of the humbler creatures. Every realm of nature is marvelous: and as Heraclitus, when the strangers who came to visit him found him warming himself at the furnace in the kitchen and hesitated to go in, is reported to have bidden them not to be afraid to enter, as even in that kitchen divinities were present, so we should venture on the study of every kind of creature without distaste; for each and all will reveal to us something natural and something beautiful. Absence of haphazard and conduciveness of everything to an end are to be found in nature's works in the highest degree, and the resultant end of her generations and combinations is a form of the beautiful.

—ARISTOTLE, *Parts of Animals*, I.5

LOVE
AND ITS PLACE
IN NATURE

1

Introduction

To start a revolution is, whether one likes it or not, to let things get out of control. Freud was a revolutionary. He unleashed a set of ideas, a way of looking at people and a way of treating them that changed the world. There must, then, be a deep sense in which he did not know what he was doing. This is not a failing on Freud's part. It is in the nature of things that one cannot both give birth to a revolution and then be there at the end of that process to appreciate its consequences. Psychic health, Freud discovered, depends on abandoning the fantasy that one can be one's own child. This is as true within the realm of thought as it is within the family.

I do not pretend to be looking back at Freud with the wisdom of the ages. It seems to me that we still do not know what he was doing. For his revolution contained three related elements whose significance we have only begun to understand: a science of subjectivity; the discovery of an archaic form of mental functioning; the positing of Love as a basic force in nature. To take these ideas seriously would be to view the world very differently than we do now.

The idea of a science of subjectivity seems, at first, paradoxical: how could there be an objective study of subjectivity? And yet, Freud realized, there had to be such a study if we were to understand human existence. For human reality is significantly constituted by subjectivity: *what it is* to be a person is shaped by *what it is like* for that person to be. The meanings, emotions and desires alive in a person's soul play a crucial role in determining who that person is. There cannot, then, be a science of human life without its including subjectivity within its scope. That is not easy to do. For, as Freud realized, the deeper meanings which shape a person's soul and structure his outlook are not immediately available to his awareness.[1] A person is, by his nature, out of touch with his own subjectivity. Thus one cannot find out what it is like for a person to be just by asking. Even if he is sincere, he won't know the answer. The only way to get at these deeper meanings is through a peculiar human interaction, the likes of which never before existed in the

---

1. Unless I am specifically referring to a male, "he" should be understood as meaning "he or she," etc. The following observation about the problem of gender pronouns made by David Velleman in *Practical Reflection* strikes me as apt:

"Some readers may take offense at my use of 'he' to denote the arbitrary person. Let me assure these readers that I share their goal of inclusiveness in language and differ with them only about the means to that goal. My view is that traditional usage in this case makes English more inclusive, not less.

"The rule governing traditional usage is that when 'he' denotes the arbitrary person, its gender is purely grammatical, not semantic, and hence carries no implications as to the referent's sex. So understood, 'he' no more denotes a man, because of being masculine, than the German 'die Person' or the French 'la personne' denotes a woman, because of being feminine.

"The alternative practices that are currently recommended as inclusive—such as saying 'he or she' or alternating 'he' with 'she'—actually threaten to rob the language of its capacity for gender-neutral reference to persons."

Let me say a word about the soul. "Soul" is a literal translation of the Greek *psyche*, and I mean no more by it than that. Insofar as psychoanalysis is an analysis of the psyche, it must, by the same token, be an analysis of the soul. In particular, there is no need to assume that the soul is separable from the body, that it is immortal, etc. (For Aristotle, for example, the soul is a principle of organization and functioning of living things. This principle is necessarily instantiated in a body.) Throughout this book I shall use "soul" and "psyche" interchangeably.

world. It is in the structured setting of a psychoanalytic therapy that the deeper strata of a person's subjectivity emerge.

If this is so, the conception of science into which Freud was born and to which he tenaciously adhered must be inadequate for the study of human life. For that conception requires that an observer remain detached from and non-intrusive with respect to the reality he is observing. This is a conception of observation that was worked out in the study of purely physical objects. There was no question of trying to capture the subjectivity of those objects: they had none. And the demand that an observer be detached gave content to the idea that he was investigating a reality that exists independently of the investigation.[2] Now, the analytic situation is, of its essence, therapeutic. There have been no interesting psychoanalytic observations of human nature that have not arisen out of an attempt to ease human suffering. Analytic therapy demands that the analyst embody a unique blend of empathy, sympathy and distance. Psychoanalysis is nothing if not a (special) emotional relationship between analyst and analysand.

Freud, it is fair to say, never worked through this conflict. As a practitioner, he was a therapist who helped himself to empathic understanding; as a theorist, he tried to fit psychoanalysis into the scientific image of his day. He never came to grips with the full force of the idea of a science of subjectivity. Neither have we. And that is why, it seems to me, most criticisms and defenses of the validity of psychoanalysis are beside the point. For the point cannot be to show that psychoanalysis does or does not conform to this

2. Cp. Williams' discussion of the absolute conception of reality in *Descartes: The Project of Enquiry*, pp. 65–67, 211–12, 245–49, 301–3. See also Clarke, "The Legacy of Skepticism."

model of science.[3] A more promising strategy is to say that the idea of a science of subjective reality is so new that we do not have any fixed model to which it should conform. Indeed, the idea of a science of subjectivity—like the idea of the unconscious mental—is at first so strange as to seem almost a contradiction in terms. If one listens carefully, one can hear the faint echoes of Viennese professors proving the unconscious mental absurd: "The mental," I hear them saying, "*must be conscious!*" Rather than take up a similarly antiquated stand with respect to the ideas of our time, we should leave ourselves open to the possibility of a science of subjectivity. Antecedently to the working out of psychoanalysis, we have little idea of what it would be to study subjectivity objectively. If we can conceive of psychoanalysis as a science of the first person, the I, we must conceive of Freud as standing at the beginning of this science, not at its end.

In trying to understand human subjectivity, mind is trying to grasp its own activity. How does mind recognize itself? That is a question which psychoanalysis raises, for Freud's great discovery is not of the unconscious per se, but of an archaic level of mental functioning that is, at first, so alien as to be unrecognizable. We are by now at home with the idea of a person having wishes, desires, fears of which he is unaware and which are not immediately available to him. What remains unsettling is that an unconscious wish is not merely an idea that lies hidden from view. The unconscious wish is expressed in dreams, in slips of the tongue,

3. See, e.g., Grunbaum, *The Foundations of Psychoanalysis*. The tendentiousness of this book's account of Freud has been well described in Sachs's "In Fairness to Freud."

in symptomatic acts, in a paralyzed leg, a false pregnancy, an irritable bowel. How is the mind to recognize itself in, say, an act of vomiting? The real mystery is not "the mysterious leap from mind to body": how something mental, an idea, can cause something physical, like vomiting, to occur.[4] The real mystery is how it is possible for there to have been no leap. How could vomiting itself be "thinking"?[5] How could we recognize the mental in something so physical?

The answer lies in the fact that recognition tends to have a transformative effect. An interpretation attempts to elucidate the content of this archaic mental activity by expressing it in terms of the higher-level thinking with which we are familiar. But this interpretation not only explicates the primitive mental activity, it can transform it. It is as though the archaic "thinking" is an early stage of a developmental process en route toward expression in terms of concepts and judgments. When the mind finally reaches an interpretation of its own activities, it can start to rework and even slough off these earlier formulations. It is the responsiveness of this archaic mental activity to the mind's own attempt to understand it that lends credibility to the idea that what we have here is a form of mental functioning. Freud noticed this responsiveness in his earliest work with hysterics, as we shall see in the next chapter, on catharsis, but one can view his entire psychoanalytic journey as an attempt to work out in detail what this responsiveness is.

Freud discovered archaic thinking in the concrete images and loose associations of dreams and in the physical symp-

---

4. Cp. Deutsch, ed., *On the Mysterious Leap from the Mind to the Body.*

5. See, e.g., Freud, "On Negation," XIX:235–39. Unless otherwise noted, all references to Freud are to *The Standard Edition of the Complete Psychological Works of Sigmund Freud.*

toms of hysterics. But because he was a scientist of his day, he could not fully appreciate its significance. A scientist, for Freud, was a discoverer of an independently existing reality. Thus he took his interpretations of unconscious motivation to be discoveries of what was *already there* in the patient's mind, causing the concrete images and the physical symptoms. This put Freud in a difficult conceptual position, and he clearly felt the strain. For if the archaic "thinking" is a remnant of infantile life, it seems odd that it should be caused by something so mature as a conceptual judgment of the type expressed in an analytic interpretation. A more compelling picture is to see the interpretation as growing naturally out of the archaic "thinking" it interprets. A good interpretation represents the end of a developmental process which begins with archaic attempts "to say the same thing." The interpretation allows the mind to understand, at the level of a conceptualized judgment, what it has been trying to say all along, in more primitive ways. Insofar as there is a natural developmental thrust by which the mind moves from archaic to more sophisticated formulations, the mind must be striving to understand its own activities. Thanks to Freud, it is by now well known that this thrust toward self-understanding is blocked by myriad inhibiting forces, which freeze much of the mind's activity at archaic levels.

A good psychoanalytic interpretation, then, does more than uncover itself. For an unconscious thought is not a fully conceptualized judgment, needing to be pulled through the looking glass by its conscious image. At least one of the reasons an unconscious thought is unconscious is that conscious mind does not easily recognize this form of mental activity. An interpretation takes up the dreams, bodily symptoms and symptomatic acts in which, say, a wish is archaically expressed, and offers the concepts with which that wish can be consciously understood. What we call an "unconscious thought" tends to be a conscious, conceptualized judgment that stands in a developmental relation to a more archaic, preconceptualized form of mental activity that is genuinely unconscious. The unconscious needs to be developed to be recognized as such. Although Freud's psychoanalytic practice embodies this developmental approach, this is not his theoretical self-understanding. Many, though not all, of his remarks suggest that he conceived of himself as simply uncovering a hidden thought. This, of course, fits with the image of science as discovering an independently existing reality.

But if we accept that an interpretation stands at the end of a developmental process, this will profoundly affect our conception of what it is for the mind to understand itself. For example, if the task of psychoanalysis is, as Freud says, to render the unconscious conscious, this requires a transformation of thinking that is not obviously conceptual into thinking that is. And there is always a danger of loss. When Socrates learned from the Delphic oracle that there was no one wiser than he, he set out to examine the wise and the gifted.[6] Here is his report of his encounters with the poets:

> I used to pick up what I thought were some of their most perfect works and question them closely about the meaning of what they had written, in the hope of incidentally enlarging my own knowledge. Well, gentlemen, I hesitate to tell you the truth, but it must be told. It is hardly an exaggeration to say that any of the bystanders could have explained those poems better than their actual authors. So I soon made up my mind about the poets too. I decided that it was not

6. See Plato, *Apology*, 21a–22d.

wisdom that enabled them to write their poetry, but
a kind of instinct or inspiration, such as you find in
seers and prophets who deliver all their sublime mes-
sages without knowing in the least what they mean.[7]

For Socrates, understanding and wisdom require that one
be able to express one's thoughts in conceptualized explanations. But can one doubt that the attempt to offer an
explanation of, say, *Oedipus Rex* entails a loss of depth,
texture, emotional vividness?[8] If any of the bystanders could
have explained the poems better than their authors, one
might think: so much the worse for explanation. Isn't Socrates, and the philosophy he represents, according too privileged a place to explanation—that is, isn't conceptual
thinking according too privileged a place to itself? For it is
only from the Socratic perspective that the poets' inability
looks like a lack of wisdom. Conceptual thinking recognizes
nothing so easily as itself, and thus there is a danger that
Socrates is blaming poetry for the difficulty of rendering it
into that form.

Does psychoanalysis share this Socratic prejudice? After
all, psychoanalysis is committed to rendering the instinctual
manifestations of human life in conceptualized interpretations. However, although an interpretation does tend to
transform that which it interprets, it does not replace it
altogether. The material which the interpretation interprets,
the "lower level" thinking, itself infuses the concepts of the
interpretation and gives them meaning and life. The idea
of the Oedipus complex permeates Western culture, yet we
remain all but ignorant of it. For the concepts that express

---

7. *Apology*, 22b–c.
8. One has only to look at Aristotle's account of the plots of tragedies. See
Poetics, esp. 17, 1455b.

it are, on their own, empty casks. Until a person is able to fill up those concepts with their manifestations in his own life, his understanding of those concepts will be hollow.

This is a different picture of the relation between concepts and objects than we are used to. Because we tend to think of mind as coming to understand an independently existing reality, we regard the concepts with which we think as distinct from the objects we think about. Mind, on this picture, comes to understand a world that exists *anyway*.[9] Now, with a psychoanalytic interpretation, by contrast, mind is trying to understand its own activities. It is thus less paradoxical to suppose that the "object" of an interpretation, say hysterical vomiting, might be affected by these attempts to understand. For we come to see that the vomiting isn't brutely physical, and thus there is less motivation for supposing that we are dealing with two fundamentally different types of thing, mind and (mind-independent) reality. The reality that mind is trying to capture is mind itself, and in its attempt to understand itself, mind does not leave itself unaltered. The whole picture of concepts and distinct objects begins to look like an idealization when we come to the case of the mind which is a self-conceptualizing object.[10]

If we remain within the vocabulary of concepts and objects, we might say that concepts on their own are not items with which the mind can understand its own activities. That is why the bare statement of, say, the Oedipus complex is so unenlightening: the mind is not yet in possession of that with which it could understand itself. A good interpretation, then, is not just a conceptualized judgment that explicates

---

9. See Bernard Williams, *Descartes: The Project of Pure Enquiry.*
10. Cp. Taylor, "Self-Interpreting Animals." This is one of the pervasive themes of Hegel's *Phenomenology of Spirit.*

psychological phenomena, it is a unity composed of the judgment and the phenomena it rationalizes. It is only when the mind can bring together its familiar thinking with its archaic mental activity that the mind is in a position to understand itself. An interpretation brings together what had, until the interpretation, seemed like diverse phenomena: it raises them up to a new unity and allows the person to move forward in ways that would not have been possible before the interpretation. From the standpoint of the interpretation, the hitherto diverse phenomena were all striving toward expression, and the interpretation provides the completion of that process. Conversely, these diverse phenomena provide the interpretative concepts with their life and meaning. For the interpretation not only makes sense of the phenomena, it is itself the product and completion of them.

Freud came to the brink of embracing this developmental approach. Although he held on to the scientific image of his day, it is remarkable how much he was nevertheless able to see in human nature which did not fit this image. One reason Freud's theoretical speculations remain exciting is that he is always trying to catch up to observations which outstrip his ability to understand them. As his thought unfolded, he came to recognize a basic developmental force in nature. This force, which he called love, permeates the animate world and tends toward the development of ever higher and more complex unities. In the human arena, a notable manifestation of love is romantic love—but that is only one of its manifestations. For within the human realm love becomes a far-reaching psychological force: what is special about human life is that it develops in complexity and structure through the mind's own activity. Freud saw this development as fueled by love, but, as we shall see in the later chapters of this book, he did not work through the consequences of positing love as a basic force in nature. For one thing, love is not something that can be appreciated from the outside. The very activity of coming to understand love is itself a development, a unification, an act of love. Nor can one just add love to nature, alongside gravity say, as a basic force which hasn't received much attention recently. If love is a basic force, our conception of nature must be transformed. Or so I shall argue in this book.

Let me say a word about death. Freud thought that human life was inevitably conflict-ridden, and he wanted to ground that conflict in a conflict of fundamental forces. He saw love as locked in an inextricable battle with an equally fundamental force for decomposition. He called this force the death drive: a force for decomposition and return to an inanimate state which permeates every living cell. And Freud invoked the death drive to explain human aggression and destructiveness. Aggression, Freud argued, was an attempt to direct this force outward, away from the self. However, Freud admitted that the ground for postulating the death drive did not arise from within psychoanalytic observation and thinking, but from biology.[11] Within the psychoanalytic arena, Freud said, the death drive "works essentially in silence."[12] That is, Freud knew that there wasn't a shred of psychoanalytic evidence for the death drive. It is thus fair to say that Freud did not succeed in giving a distinctively psychoanalytic account of human aggression. He tried to *derive* aggression from a more fun-

---

11. Cp., e.g., *Beyond the Pleasure Principle*, XVIII:37–61; *The Ego and the Id*, XIX:40; "Two Encyclopedia Articles," XVIII:258.

12. "Two Encyclopedia Articles," XVIII:258. See also "An Autobiographical Study," XX:57; *An Outline of Psycho-Analysis*, XXIII:150; *Beyond the Pleasure Principle*, XVIII:52, 59–60. I discuss this in greater detail in Chapter 5.

damental biological source, and thus he violated his own "fundamental rule": to give a psychological account of psychological phenomena.[13] And herein lies a crucial difference between love and death: within the human realm love is itself a psychological force; death is not. Death remains a purely biological force from which psychological consequences, like aggression, are supposed to flow. For a worthy opponent to love, Freud should have chosen hate or strife: a force which in the human realm is psychological. Within the human arena, strife shouldn't *cause* strife, it should *be* strife.[14] Of course, aggression will be part of any complete psychoanalytic portrait of human nature.[15] But, equally, aggression is part of the psychoanalytic canvas that Freud left incompletely painted. Since our concern is the philosophical implications of Freudian *psychoanalysis*, there is reason to set death aside. From the point of view of psychoanalysis, the death drive is a brute Something Else with which love is locked in struggle. So even if life is inevitably a struggle between love and death, our task is to focus in on what death is struggling with. This *is* one-sided: but

13. This, one might say, is his "other" fundamental rule. See, e.g., "On Narcissism: An Introduction," XIV:78–79. Cp. "The Unconscious," XIV:174–75; *Three Essays on the Theory of Sexuality*, VII:243. I discuss the "other" fundamental rule in Chapter 5.

14. See Freud's discussion of Empedocles' principles in "Analysis Terminable and Interminable," XXIII:245–47. In fact, Empedocles' choice of love or friendship (*philia*) and strife (*neikos*) is superior to Freud's love and death, precisely because strife stays at the same level of reality as love, whereas death is confined to the biological realm.

15. Thus the task of working out a distinctively psychoanalytic account of aggression is one of the important legacies Freud bequeathed to the next generation of analysts. See, e.g., Winnicott, "Aggression in Relation to Emotional Development" and "Hate in the Countertransference," in *Through Paediatrics to Psycho-Analysis*; Anna Freud, *The Ego and the Mechanisms of Defense*; "Aggression in Relation to Emotional Development," *Psychoanalytic Study of the Child*, III–IV, 1947; Klein, "A Contribution to the Theory of Intellectual Inhibition" and "Early Stages of the Oedipus Conflict," in *Love, Guilt and Reparation*; "Some Theoretical Conclusions Regarding the Emotional Life of the Infant," in *Envy and Gratitude*.

the problem with being one-sided arises when one pretends to be giving the whole story. I claim only to be looking at deeper layers of that part of the Freudian canvas which is psychoanalytic through and through.[16] There is, I suspect, something healthy about doing this, for love has become almost taboo within psychoanalysis. Analysts talk of sex and aggression with ease, but as soon as anyone starts to talk of love, from somewhere there instantly comes the response: But what about aggression? This would be reason enough for love to command our attention.

This book is an interpretation. As such, it is an act of love. It does not claim to find the hidden meaning in Freud, as though this meaning was lurking there, already existing, below the manifest level of the text. It is, rather, an attempt to develop some significant strains in Freudian psychoanalytic thinking. An attempt to bring together and unify disparate elements in Freudian thought and to find a unity in those elements that was not immediately evident. From the standpoint of this interpretation, it looks as though Freudian thinking was striving in this direction. That is, this book attempts to offer a developmental interpretation of Freudian psychoanalysis. It does not try to do justice to everything Freud says, or to capture Freud's own understanding of psychoanalysis, or to uncover what is "really there." Rather, it takes up and develops certain salient themes in Freud, themes that from the perspective of this interpretation are his theoretically symptomatic acts. It pursues connections, insights, consequences of Freudian thoughts that Freud himself did not pursue, and of which

---

16. I hope in a future work to discuss the psychoanalytic understanding of the role of aggression in human development.

he remained unaware. In this sense, the book is about the Freudian unconscious.

This book, then, is an interpretation in very much the same sense as a psychoanalytic interpretation is. Thus we need not conceive of ourselves as detached observers investigating a subject matter which is set *out there*, existing independently of our investigation. This is a book *about* psychoanalytic theory, but it is also a piece of psychoanalytic theorizing. Psychoanalytic theory is the "object" of the inquiry, but inquiring into this "subject matter" does not require holding it at arm's length. In fact, the claim is stronger. If psychoanalysis is a healthy activity, we could not possibly come to understand it by holding it at arm's length. For if psychoanalytic interpretation is as rich and enriching an activity as it takes itself to be, then any understanding-bequeathing interpretation of it will naturally tend also to be an instance and manifestation of it. This does not immediately seal the fate on the possibility of an objective understanding of psychoanalysis. There is no unproblematic notion of objectivity that can simply be applied to determine whether or not our investigation is "objective."

Similarly, psychoanalytic theorizing cannot properly be conceived as detached from psychoanalytic practice. The concepts of theory, if they are to earn their theoretical living, are infused with meaning by the daily efforts of analysts and analysands, trying to come to grips with, to understand and react to, their lives, their sufferings and, sometimes, their joys. Psychoanalytic concepts must be grounded in the activities of human beings for them to have any life. Conversely, psychoanalytic practice is grounded in the belief that it is possible for people to absorb psychoanalytic concepts into their souls and that this absorption may enable them to transform the way they live. This does not mean that a successful analysis requires that the analysand become a psychoanalytic theorist; it means only that he is capable of absorbing and making use of good interpretations. Just as the philosophical study of psychoanalytic theory cannot be detached from psychoanalytic theory, so psychoanalytic theory cannot be detached from psychoanalytic practice. All of this just is: psychoanalysis.

Let me at once admit, though, that I want to use the distinction between theory and practice as a useful conceit. I would like to distinguish between Freud's "practice" of psychoanalysis as he himself describes it in the case studies and clinical vignettes that pepper his work, and his theorizing about his practice. His theorizing would include his models of the mind, his conceptualization of the unconscious, of drives, etc. His clinical descriptions are so rich that they provide us with the material to develop a better conceptualization of what Freud was doing than he could provide for himself. This is not a criticism of Freud so much as a reevaluation. Let me put it in terms that Freud might have found pleasing. Freud was committed to science—that is, to science as he understood it. One of the hallmarks of great science is that it lends itself to future development. It is not a reasonable ideal for even a great scientist to want his discoveries to remain forever unmodified by future generations. Newton is not diminished in stature because the world has since been discovered to operate according to non-Newtonian principles. If we are to treat psychoanalysis as a science and Freud as a scientist, we must not approach his texts as holy writ. What we have here is a first, brilliant attempt of humans to come to understand themselves in certain ways. We must take up his work, interpret it, reevaluate it, if psychoanalysis is to be a living activity. We must *work through* Freud.

That is what this book does: it takes certain Freudian texts more or less chronologically and shows how psychoanalysis unfolds from its own conflicts. The unresolved tensions within psychoanalysis provide an inner dynamic of growth. Psychoanalysis, one might say, is itself on the couch: and the aim of this book is to construct a vibrant conceptual history—an interpretation of the psychic life of the analysand—that helps psychoanalysis to live.

Psychoanalysis, many have claimed, is dying. To my mind, the issue is not whether psychoanalysis is obsolete, but whether the individual is. The commitment to the individual is a tradition in the West, and psychoanalysis is itself a manifestation of that commitment. But it is easy to misunderstand what this commitment is, and there is a significant reason why this misunderstanding occurs. Consider, by way of analogy, the obsessional who endlessly debates whether or not he is in love. Every facet of his lover's personality will be held up to the light, only to be taken to the light once again. To the obsessional, it looks as though his inquiry spans the universe of options—either he is in love or he is not—and in his never-ending pursuit of the answer, no stone is left unturned.[17] In fact, the debate disguises the real issue, for it assumes that he is capable of love.[18] That is the underlying assumption which his ambivalence hides and protects. What looked like an exhaustive debate turns out to be merely exhausting.

This obsessional strategy can permeate a culture. It is by

17. Sometimes literally: see Freud's account of the Rat Man, "Notes upon a Case of Obsessional Neurosis," X:190–91.

18. See Wollheim's fascinating discussion of the Narrator's investigation of whether he loves Albertine in Proust's *A la Recherche du Temps Perdu* (*The Thread of Life*, pp. 191–92).

now a commonplace that the modern West is concerned with the individual. Some think this is good, others that it is bad. Those in favor think that Western societies allow the individual to pursue his desires just so long as he doesn't interfere with the legitimate interests of others. Those against think that individuals are encouraged to be self-indulgent: all those aerobic classes and Nautilus machines, those self-help books and luxury vacations numb us to our responsibilities to society and to humanity. In reaction, one sees people turning to Eastern religions and philosophies which do not stress the individual. But to debate whether or not our concern with the individual is a good thing is to assume that we are a group of individuals. Are we? Is it possible that the entire debate over individual*ism*, pro and con, proceeds by ignoring the individual? Certainly, individualistic political philosophies, while paying great attention to individual rights and liberties, tend to remain silent on what individuals are. Individuals are treated as atoms, with little notice given to subatomic structure. But then it seems there could be an individualistic society full of members pursuing their own interests while the society as a whole frustrates the development of individuals. An individualistic society with no individuals!

Therein lies the problem with self-help books: selves are not that easy to help. An individual requires a kind of nurturing and growth that goes far beyond aerobics and quick-fix therapy. We can all imagine someone whose muscle tone is great, who is successful at his job, who "feels good about himself" and yet remains a shell of a human being.[19] However relentless that person is in the pursuit of his desires,

---

19. See, e.g., Winnicott, "Ego Distortion in Terms of True and False Self," in *The Maturational Processes and the Facilitating Environment*; Miller, *The Drama of the Gifted Child*.

there seems to be something wrong with thinking of such a person as selfish. There does not yet seem to be a self on the scene capable of selfishness or selflessness.[20] Who, after all, has set this particular conception of physical fitness as a measure of self-esteem; who has determined the model of success; who, indeed, has put forward the picture of what it is to "feel good" about oneself? It becomes tenuous to think of this person as pursuing *his* desires. One symptom of our age is that we live with a caricatured conception of eccentricity. There is, of course, the absentminded professor combing a musty study for the glasses which are sitting on top of his nose; there is the British eccentric of the nineteenth century, butterfly net in hand . . . etc. These distorted images disguise from us the fact that a true eccentric is simply someone who is moving in a different orbit from everyone else. A true eccentric is someone who has tried to determine what his desires and values are, to make them his own, and to live by them: by his very nature, an eccentric is not willing simply to conform to culturally given standards of "self-fulfillment." Even if he ends up participating in a culture's values—even if his orbit is a minor perturbation of tradition—he will make those values distinctively his own. The very idea that an eccentric is a deviation suggests that we are, by and large, concentrics.

Here it is worth comparing psychoanalysis with more drug-oriented approaches to psychiatry. To what extent does psychopharmacology promote concentricity? There is nothing at its core that forces it to. The truly remarkable ability of drugs to spring someone out of a depression, calm a florid psychotic episode, manage a manic-depressive cycle,

---

20. Cp. Kohut, *The Analysis of the Self.*

can help people on their ways to living the unique lives of which they are capable. My criticism is not directed toward psychopharmacology, but toward a certain cultural image of what that treatment can accomplish. On this image, neurological and pharmacological research, if not now, will soon render in-depth psychotherapy obsolete. That this is a powerful image is undoubted: generations of psychiatrists are being trained with, at best, the most rudimentary exposure to psychotherapeutic techniques. And yet, for all their immense value in relieving human suffering, there is no evidence that drugs, surgery or electroconvulsive therapy can treat more than the grossest of psychic phenomena. That there will be marvelous advances in neurology and pharmacology is beyond question; that they will solve the conflicts inherent in living *this* particular life is fantasy. And however valuable it may be to jump-start someone out of a depression, from the point of view of our commitment to the individual, the all-important question is: what happens next? Does the person use the relief from crippling pain as an opportunity to work through the meanings and conflicts inherent in his life; or is he "relieved" of that opportunity? This is ultimately the question of whether a person is freed *to* become an individual—or "freed" *from* that possibility. Individuation is a process that begins at birth and can continue at ever higher levels of development throughout life. It is precisely by pursuing the meanings by which a life is lived that a person takes up again the process of differentiation from parents and the social world, a process which, for one reason or another, may have stalled. No drug can take the place of this pursuit. For the pursuit of meaning is not a *means* by which an individual comes to be: as though someday other means may be discovered or invented. An individual is, among other things, *constituted* by the pursuit of the meanings by which he does or might live.

Psychoanalysis is at its core committed to the process of individuation; and it will flourish or wither depending on the value we place on the individual and the development of individuals in society. Do we, as a culture, want more from psychiatry and psychotherapy than to get a person back to work, get a person back to (or out of) his family in the cheapest, most efficient way? Do we wish to do more than damp down anxiety? I do not know how to answer these questions, but I am convinced that psychoanalysis will stand or fall with our culture's commitment to the individual.

Psychoanalysis did not begin with this self-understanding: it had to discover this about itself. In fact, *it is in the individual that the three elements of Freud's revolution—subjectivity, archaic mind and love—come together*. It is precisely because even a mature individual never leaves archaic life completely behind that a person's subjectivity permeates his being. His outlook is not exhausted by his conscious thoughts but spreads throughout his existence. Even bodily functioning is an expression of a person's subjectivity: there is not a physical organ that we can say with confidence is unaffected. Moreover, psychoanalysis discovered that individual freedom requires freedom to become an individual. Since a person is significantly constituted by his subjectivity, one cannot legitimately assume that a biological unit, a member of the human species, is an individual. For part of what it is to be an individual is to take oneself to be one: to distinguish oneself from the environment in which one lives. Being an individual, psychoanalysis discovered, is a psychological achievement; for the ability to distinguish oneself from the environment is not present at the beginning of biological or psychic life. Precisely because the individual is a psychological achievement, it is not a given and cannot be taken for granted. But for an individual to come into existence, his archaic expression of subjectivity must be integrated into the rest of his life. An individual comes to be not by abolishing archaic life, but by taking it up into a higher level of organization. Freud, as we shall see, came to recognize this development as a manifestation of love within the human arena.

For an individual to come to be, he needs freedom from certain internal and external tyrannies. Internally, the individual may be tyrannized by subindividual psychic forces, which Freud called "drives," which may threaten and overwhelm the psychological integrity of the individual. It is the task of individual development, as it is the task of psychoanalysis, to promote a healthy relation between an individual and his drives—a "healthy" relation being, from this perspective, one that promotes the growth and development of the individual.

Externally, the individual may be threatened by these very same drives, now located in the social world. It is by now a commonplace that, for Freud, civilization forces man to become neurotic. Of course, much of what Freud says on man in society is consonant with this picture, but there is a darker and deeper picture that also bubbles to the surface of his work. If the individual is a psychic achievement, and if the drives are the pre-individualized elements of psychic life, then there is the possibility of a social group composed of proto-individuals: a We that is not a collection of I's. This is what Freud called a mass, and it should be distinguished from a group of individuals, for mass psychology is essentially the psychology of the drives located in the social

world.[21] Mass psychology threatens the individual in two
ways. First, the mass is hostile to the individual. At his trial,
Socrates said that what would secure his destruction was
not his formal accusers or their speeches, but a long-smol-
dering hostility of the group.[22] And what had Socrates done
other than to promote his own brand of psychoanalysis: to
encourage each citizen to look inside his soul and examine
his beliefs? Socrates was guilty of promoting the development of individual conscience, of furthering individualiza-
tion in Athenian society, and he knew that he would be
convicted not on the basis of reason or argument, but on
the basis of rumor, suspicion and mass hostility. The fact
that the specific charges brought against him were un-
founded counted for little, as Socrates well knew. And yet,
mass mind came to the right verdict, at least by its own
lights. For the idea of a society of individuals—a We that
is a group of I's—must be inimical to a society that depends
on mass psychology for its continued existence. By his
death, Socrates showed that Athenian democracy could not
sustain its commitment to the idea of democracy.

The second way in which mass psychology threatens the
individual is by its attraction. Since the individual carries
his psychic past within him, there is an ever-present tendency to regress to pre-individual forms of life. A mob is
powerful because it can encourage this regression: the activity of mass mind is itself an inducement to regress and
join in. It would seem then that the idea of a society of

---

21. See, especially, *Group Psychology and the Analysis of the Ego*, XVIII:65–
143. (Freud draws heavily here on Le Bon's *Psychologie des Foules*.) A better
translation of the title *Massenpsychologie und Ich-Analyse* might be "Mass Psychology and I-Analysis," for Freud is here concerned with a particular type of
group: a group of non-individuals which we more comfortably refer to as a mass
or a mob.
22. Plato, *Apology*, 18a–c, 22e–23a, 28a–b.

individuals is to some extent an idealization. For each individual carries within him pre-individual psychic forces and these will be in play even in relatively individualized societies. The question then is not whether these forces have been abolished, but whether they have been deployed in such a way that an individual can stand in a healthy relation to his society. Here again, "health" is from the perspective of the individual: the relation is healthy *if* society allows and promotes the growth and flourishing of the individual.

Psychoanalysis has discovered that individuals are not part of the basic fabric of the world, not even of the basic fabric of human society. That individuals exist depends on the social world nurturing their development, and this is a contingent matter. We live in an age that tends to believe, almost without argument, in cultural and historical relativism. What present themselves as basic truths are, from a relativist perspective, only artifacts of a particular culture or historical age. The apparent necessity of these truths only signifies, from a relativist perspective, that we cannot (yet) see beyond the bounds of our time and culture.[23] Relativism seems most unsettling when it is directed onto our values. Consider, for example, the claim that although *we* value individual freedom or autonomy, it is only from within this perspective that a society committed to freedom of the individual looks better than a society that is not. It is hard to know how to answer such a challenge. On the one hand, any straightforward answer explaining the value of individual freedom would be dismissed as one more embellishment of our time, part of the original cultural package that this challenge is calling into question. But, on the other hand, there seems to be nothing else we could possibly say, for

---

23. Remember our Viennese professors.

there is no way to step outside our time and culture and view it from an absolutely neutral perspective.

Psychoanalysis is of help here. Without trying to ascend to a godlike perspective, it gives us a vivid sense of the cost of abandoning the modern commitment to the individual. Psychoanalysis teaches us that the existence of an individual is not coincident with the existence of a human being, but depends on the human's having grown up in a favorable social environment. The lesson of this contingency, however, is not that "anything goes," but that *we* go. For it is not that if we were in a culture not committed to the individual, life would be very different for us (though not necessarily worse from the perspective of that culture). For we, in the sense of a group of I's, would not survive the transition to that culture. The cultural transformation would require the abandonment of the psychological achievement of individuation, and since the individual is actually constituted by this achievement, it would mean the end of the individual. The group would degenerate into a mass. To assume that *we* would continue on, though in a different sort of life, is like the fantasy of experiencing one's own death.[24]

But who are *we*? That is the question psychoanalysis sets out to answer, preserving the first-personal accent in the answer that is there in the question. It is grounded in the belief that in the peculiarities of the first-personal, subjective experience of human suffering, it can delineate broad-scale features of the human condition, of what it is to be us. Thucydides wrote his *History of the Peloponnesian War* not just to give an account of those particular battles. He be-

---

24. Actually, psychoanalysis does lend insight into what this "death" might be like, for it allows us to appreciate the non-individuated aspects of our psychic lives.

lieved that the only way he could provide deep insight into the nature of human existence was via a detailed history of that war. Psychoanalysis is the history of a series of battles that are fought and refought within the human soul. And Freud could have said of his case histories what Thucydides said of his *History*: "I have written my work, not as an essay which is to win the applause of the moment, but as a possession for all time."[25]

Now, though there are classic human battles, life is not condemned to repetition. For Freud discovered in the heart of these battles at least the potential for human growth. And while the development of an individual may be a *contingency*, Freud also discovered that this development is not *arbitrary*. Of course, Freud's attention is primarily focused on the pathologies of development, rather than on the healthy trajectories. And, in his vision, human life is inevitably conflict-ridden. However, insofar as he traced the route of love as it is manifested in human beings, Freud saw that it was a force for individuation. So though a society of individuals may or may not emerge in human history, its emergence is, from Freud's perspective, not just an accident. There is, for him, a basic force in nature promoting this development.

Psychoanalysis, Freud once said, is a cure through love.[26] On the manifest level, Freud meant that psychoanalytic therapy requires the analysand's emotional engagement with the analyst and the analyst's empathic understanding of his patient. But the latent content of this remark, which Freud only gradually discovered, and then through a glass darkly, is that psychoanalysis in its essence promotes individuation.

---

25. *History of the Peloponnesian War*, I.1. This issue is discussed in Farrar, *The Origins of Democratic Thinking*.

26. Letter to Jung, December 6, 1906, *The Freud/Jung Letters*, pp. 12–13.

In that sense, psychoanalysis is itself a manifestation of love. And the emergence of psychoanalysis onto the human scene must, from this perspective, be part of love's developmental history. Freud cannot, then, legitimately conceive of himself as a detached observer of the struggle between love and death in human life, for his very thinking and therapeutic activity must be an expression of (at least) one of the forces he is trying to observe. Of course, all this talk of love and death may seem quaint, even embarrassing. The embarrassment is, I suspect, a symptom that we are treading in intellectually threatening territory. Much easier, then, to dismiss Freud's mature theory of the drives as a speculative excrescence. Much more difficult to work through the consequences of this theory to discover that he is a more radical thinker than we, or he, suspected.

2

Catharsis:
Fantasy and Reality

I

Subjectivity is upwardly mobile. The meanings and memories that shape a person's outlook on the world do not lie dormant in the soul; they are striving for expression. Psychoanalysis, Freud suggests, began with "a chance observation."[1] These are the first words of the *Studies on Hysteria*, and the "chance observation," made by Freud's colleague Breuer, was that his patient Anna O. could obtain both physical and psychic relief if, in a hypnotic state, she "talked herself out."[2] This talking often consisted in her imaginative products of the day, but regularly her talking led her back to memories that seemed to lie at the heart of her problem. Let us consider one of Breuer's more striking descriptions:

> It was in the summer during a period of extreme heat, and the patient was suffering very badly from thirst;

1. *Studies on Hysteria*, II:3.
2. *Studies on Hysteria*, II:27.

for, without being able to account for it in any way, she suddenly found it impossible to drink. She would take up the glass of water she longed for, but as soon as it touched her lips she would push it away like someone suffering from hydrophobia. As she did this, she was obviously in an *absence* for a couple of seconds. She lived only on fruit, such as melons, etc., so as to lessen her tormenting thirst. This had lasted for some six weeks, when one day during hypnosis she grumbled about her English lady-companion whom she did not care for, and went on to describe, with every sign of disgust, how she had once gone into that lady's room and how her little dog—horrid creature!—had drunk out of a glass there. The patient had said nothing, as she had wanted to be polite. After giving further energetic expression to the anger she had held back, she asked for something to drink, drank a large quantity of water without any difficulty and woke up from her hypnosis with the glass at her lips; and thereupon the disturbance vanished, never to return.[3]

The "chance observation" was not only that "talking herself out" brought relief; it almost inevitably led back to a memory that could legitimately be considered the cause of the symptom. Before the memory was recovered, the symptom persisted; as soon as it was recovered, the symptom vanished. So while it may have been chance that Breuer ever sat down and listened to Anna O., once he did so, it was hardly chance that he made this observation. Anna O.'s subjectivity was dying for expression. This discovery spawned a technical procedure.

3. *Studies on Hysteria*, II:34–35.

These findings—that in the case of this patient the hysterical phenomena disappeared as soon as the event which had given rise to them was reproduced in her hypnosis—made it possible to arrive at a therapeutic technical procedure which left nothing to be desired in its logical consistency and systematic application. Each individual symptom in this complicated case was taken separately in hand; all the occasions on which it had appeared were described in reverse order, starting before the time when the patient became bedridden and going back to the event which had led to its first appearance. When this had been described, the symptom was permanently removed.[4]

Freud and Breuer together discovered that this procedure could be generalized. Over and over again, they discovered that their lame, paralyzed, anesthetic, vomiting patients were in fact being tyrannized by a memory of which they were unaware. "Hysterics," as they famously put it, "suffer mainly from reminiscences."[5]

But why did the memories tyrannize? Freud and Breuer suggest that it is because the events of which they are memories were not lived properly. When Anna O. discovered the dog drinking out of the glass she did not express her disgust because she wanted to be polite. That unexpressed disgust seemed to take up residence in her: and it became responsible for a generalized disgust of drinking. Or, to take one of Freud's cases, Fräulein Elisabeth von R. fell in love with her brother-in-law but did not allow herself to experience her emotion. At the very moment she arrived at her

---

4. *Studies on Hysteria*, II:35.
5. *Studies on Hysteria*, II:7.

sister's deathbed, too late to bid her farewell, she found herself involuntarily thinking, "Now he is free again and I can be his wife."[6] But this thought quickly left her consciousness. As Freud put it: "She succeeded in sparing herself the painful conviction that she loved her sister's husband, by inducing physical pains in herself instead."[7] What seems to have happened in both these cases is that an appropriate emotional reaction was stifled because, to put it paradoxically, it was inappropriate.

The emotional reaction was appropriate because it was a manifestation of how the person really felt. It was inappropriate because it was socially unacceptable. It was impolite for Anna O. freely to express her disgust; it was embarrassing and shameful for Elisabeth von R. to confess even to herself, let alone declare, her love for her sister's husband. In each case there seems to be a conflict between the person's emotional orientation to the world and the demands that the person supposes the world to be making on her. The site of the conflict is not the frontier between person and world: it is within the person. It is because Elisabeth had herself accepted societal values about kinship that she found her love shameful and embarrassing. These internalized values could not only cause shame, they could make the love disappear. But, Freud discovered, this was a case in which out of sight did not mean out of mind. In some sense the love persisted, unacknowledged, unaware, causing physical symptoms.

Freud's conception of hysteria was determined by its cure. As Freud and Breuer put it in their preliminary communication:

---

6. *Studies on Hysteria*, II:156.
7. *Studies on Hysteria*, II:157.

. . . we found, to our great surprise at first, that *each individual hysterical symptom immediately and permanently disappeared when we had succeeded in bringing clearly to light the memory of the event by which it was provoked and in arousing its accompanying emotion, and when the patient had described that event in the greatest possible detail and had put the emotion into words.* Recollection without emotion almost invariably produces no result.[8]

Since the expression of the emotion was therapeutic, it was natural for Freud and Breuer to conceive of their method as a type of discharge. Before the treatment the emotion persisted "inside" the patient, causing the hysterical symptoms; the treatment consisted in expelling this "foreign body."[9] But while it is natural so to conceive their treatment, it is by no means necessary for them to do so. What Freud and Breuer seem to describe as therapeutic is a conscious unification of thought and feeling. For what is meant by "putting the emotion into words" is the unification of a conscious appreciation of a significant past experience with an emotional response that is, for them, a genuine response. The problem with hysterics is that at the time of the traumatic experience they found themselves unable to experience such a response. This breach between experience and

8. *Studies on Hysteria*, II:6 (their emphasis). The Standard Edition translates *Affekt* as "affect" rather than as "emotion." This preserves similarity in spelling and sound, but is otherwise unfortunate, for the English word, with this meaning, is rarely used in contemporary English. Now, one could preserve the translation and then ask a question like "How do affects correspond to emotions?" but a question like this, I think, helps to disguise what is really at issue. For it is not as though there are two types of thing in the world, affects and emotions, and a question as to how they relate; it is, rather, that there is one type of thing in the world, emotions, and a question as to how it should best be conceptualized.

9. *Studies on Hysteria*, II:6; cp. II:165.

emotional response sets up a force in them which is causally responsible for their hysterical symptoms.

This force could only be dissipated by imaginatively reliving the experience, this time with feeling. But why conceive of this unification of thought and feeling as a discharge? Freud and Breuer speak of the memory of the trauma as a "foreign body" that continues to have a toxic effect on the patient,[10] and it was the function of traditional medical catharsis to expel foreign bodies. But the idea of the traumatic memory as a "foreign body" is itself part of the conception of discharge: it does not help to explain it. Indeed, if one asks what basis there could be for regarding any memory as a foreign body, the only reason that emerges is that these memories are split off from consciousness.[11] These traumatic memories are *alien to consciousness*, and it is in large part due to their remaining unconscious that they are able to have a pathological effect. But if a memory's remaining without citizenship in the land of consciousness is the basis for considering it a "foreign body," then the metaphor of a "foreign body" should not suggest discharge, but an opening up of the borders. For it is only by welcoming the foreign body *into* consciousness, by granting it citizenship, that its toxic effects are overcome. Freud does on occasion suggest that the therapeutic process consists in just such a unification of the split-off idea with consciousness, but he doesn't see this conception as offering an alternative to the discharge model.[12]

One reason for conceiving catharsis as a discharge is that it is natural for humans so to conceive of the expression of

---

10. *Studies on Hysteria*, II:6; cp. 165.
11. *Studies on Hysteria*, II:9–12; cp. 290.
12. See, e.g., *Studies on Hysteria*, II:124.

the emotions.[13] As Freud pointed out, this is reflected in such common linguistic usage as "to cry oneself out" or "to blow off steam."[14] Here, then, is an occupational hazard for psychoanalytic theorists. Although Breuer reported that Anna O. "aptly described" his therapeutic procedure as a "talking cure" and only "jokingly" referred to it as "chimney-sweeping," this "joke" worked its way into the theoretical formulation of catharsis. Psychoanalytic theory is, in part, an abstraction from the symptoms and verbal reports of neurotic and psychotic patients. But these verbal reports are themselves manifestations of the patients' fantasies, fantasies that psychoanalysis is trying to understand and treat. Catharsis was experienced by Anna O., at some level of her experience, as a discharge. But even if that is, *for* her, what happened, why should one assume that is what happened *to* her?

Freud had not yet discovered archaic mental functioning, so he was not in a position to see that his and Breuer's theory of catharsis was not describing a real emotional process so much as a fantasied conception of that process. The case of Anna O. shows us, right at the beginning of psychoanalysis, that in addition to infecting our memories and current experience, archaic mental life has a "theory" of the mind's own workings.[15] Anna O.'s "theory" of catharsis was

13. See, e.g., Fairbairn, "Schizoid Factors in the Personality," in *Psychoanalytic Studies of the Personality*. Fairbairn has argued that the schizoid position manifested in hysteria is the most primitive and basic human psychical organization. Thus at some level we all find it "natural" to conceive of emotions in bodily terms and ordinary linguistic usage reflects this. See also Wollheim "The Mind and the Mind's Image of Itself."

14. *Studies on Hysteria*, II:8; cp. "Psychopathic Characters on the Stage," VII:305–6.

15. Wollheim has elegantly made the point that archaic mental functioning comes with its own "archaic" theory of the mind. See, e.g., *The Thread of Life*, pp. 141–61.

not an explicitly conceptualized theory, thus the use of quotes. Her "theory" was expressed at the same archaic level of mental functioning as the rest of her fantasies: she experienced catharsis as a corporealized discharge. Freud and Breuer turned Anna O.'s "theory" into a theory. Obviously, they were deeply influenced by the scientific theories of their day—for example, the law of thermodynamics. But in formulating a theory of catharsis, they provided the concepts with which to express Anna O.'s "theory" in conscious judgments. So although they gave an account of a therapeutic treatment, they also rendered the fantasy of emotional discharge, which we all tend to share, into a conscious theory.

That is, they unwittingly provided an interpretation of Anna O.'s fantasy. What is so remarkable about this transformation from unconscious fantasied "theory" into conscious theory is that it shows us that, even in its most primitive activities, the mind is striving for self-understanding. It is as though self-consciousness is implicit in even the most primitive unconscious mental processes. For the fantasy of emotional discharge is an implicit account of the mind's own workings, an account which Freud's theory of catharsis made explicit. The theory of catharsis is thus a conceptual expression of hysterical state of mind. And yet, there is a sense in which the mind must be right about itself. Insofar as a fantasy of discharge is inherent in the process by which a person expresses an emotion and has done with it, then the mind is right that there has been a discharge. What the mind cannot be expected to know about itself, at least at this level of mental functioning, is that the discharge is a fantasied discharge. "Fantasy" is a term we apply to an experience only after we have distanced ourselves from it. Within the fantasy, the distinction between fantasy and reality does not and cannot arise.

It is because fantasies of mental functioning are present from the beginning of mental life and actually influence mental functioning that psychoanalysis can be a "talking cure." If mental functioning were as remote from a person's self-understanding as, say, brain functioning, there would be no reason to think that a person could tell us about his mental processes. But it seems that even the most archaic unconscious mental process contains within it an implicit, fantasied "theory" of that process. A "theory" of the mental process is part of the person's (perhaps unconscious) experience of that process. Thus the fantasied "theory" becomes part and parcel of the mental process, and in altering the fantasy one alters the mental process itself.

This may at first seem strange, but only because one is thinking of a fantasy along the lines of a mental image, projected on the screen of the mind. Perhaps it is our dream experiences that fuel this underlying conception of fantasy. But once one is in the grips of this conception, it becomes unclear how fantasies could exert any efficacy over mental functioning. How, after all, could an image of mental functioning affect mental functioning? Instead of trying to answer this question, one should reject the assumption on which it is based. A person's subjectivity is powerful not merely because it is striving for expression but also because it may be expressed archaically. Archaic mental functioning knows no firm boundary between mind and body, and so archaic mind is incarnate in the body. Although fantasies may be expressed in images, they may also occur in paralyses, vomiting, skin irritations, spasms, ulcers, etc.; and even by being dramatically acted out by the person whose fantasy it is. In this way a person's subjectivity permeates his being. So, for example, if a person's fantasied "theory" of catharsis is that it is an emotional purgation, this "theory" should be manifest in various aspects of that person's experience: he may feel "drained," or "depleted," "spent," "exhausted," "empty," after a cathartic emotional experience. This is the sense in which every person must have the truth within him.

Because a person is striving archaically to conform to his archaic "theory," a science of subjectivity cannot leave this archaic "theory" completely behind. For example, when a person engages in a "talking cure," he tries to give conscious, conceptualized expression to his archaic fantasies of mental functioning. In so doing, he is able to influence the fantasy and thus the mental functioning which embodies and expresses that fantasy. How is this possible? The therapeutic influence of talking would be mysterious if the analysand were simply formulating a distinct perspective on his mental life. But the analysand's talking is not so much the formulation of a detached view *of* his subjectivity as it is an expression at a higher level of the very subjectivity he is trying to understand. The analysand's emerging, conscious theory of how he goes on is thus incestuously related to his archaic "theory." The conscious, verbal account grows out of an archaic attempt "to say the same thing." The analysand, then, is not the detached observer of his subjectivity: his talking is the growth of that subjectivity.[16] And it is because talking stands in a developmental relation to its archaic forebears that it can exert some influence over them. Nothing less is at stake than the transformation of the mode in which a person's subjectivity is expressed.

---

16. Similarly, the analyst's interpretations are less a detached observation of the analysand's subjectivity than a certain development of that very subjectivity. And so a science of subjectivity will not be a detached observation of an independently existing subjectivity, but a certain development of subjectivity itself. This is a theme I shall develop throughout the rest of this book, but especially in Chapter 6.

Freud's practice of catharsis embodies this transformation, though Freud is not yet in a theoretical position to
appreciate that this is what he is doing.[17] A hysterical symptom, Freud thought, represented the *conversion* of something mental into something physical: Elisabeth von R., for
example, converted her mental pain into physical pain.[18]
Because Freud has not yet recognized archaic mental functioning, he is not yet in a position to see that no leap from
mind to body is necessary. Indeed, no leap is possible: not
because of an unbridgeable gulf between mind and body,
but because at the archaic level the body is the mind. Elisabeth von R.'s physical pain is here mental pain (archaically
expressed). But once one has the idea that a hysterical symptom is a conversion, there must be an underlying something
that can be expressed sometimes mentally, sometimes physically. This underlying something Freud conceived of as
psychic energy.

. . . we regard hysterical symptoms as the effects and
residues of excitations which have acted upon the nervous system as traumas. Residues of this kind are not
left behind if the original excitation has been discharged by abreaction or thought-activity. It is impossible any longer at this point to avoid introducing
the idea of *quantities* (even though not measurable
ones). We must regard the process as though a *sum
of excitation* impinging on the nervous system is transformed into chronic symptoms in so far as it has not
been employed for external action in proportion to its
amount. Now we are accustomed to find in hysteria
that a considerable part of this "sum of excitation" of

17. See, e.g., *Studies on Hysteria*, II:166.
18. *Studies on Hysteria*, II:157.

the trauma is transformed into purely somatic symptoms. It is this characteristic of hysteria which has so long stood in the way of its being recognized as a psychical disorder.[19]

It is important to see how Freud's scientific image is being used to legitimate a fantasied conception of mental processes. Once there is an underlying psychical energy that may manifest itself either in hysterical symptoms or in active emotional reactions, it makes sense to conceive of those emotional reactions as discharges of energy. The idea of psychical energy also answers the question of how mental pain could possibly be converted into physical pain.

We may ask: what is it that turns into physical pain here? A cautious reply would be: something that *might have become and should have become mental pain*. If we venture a little further and try to represent the ideational mechanism in a kind of algebraical picture, we may attribute a certain *quota of emotion* to the ideational complex of these erotic feelings which remained unconscious, and say that *this quantity (the quota of emotion) is what was converted*. It would follow directly from this description that the "unconscious love" would have lost so much of its intensity through a conversion of this kind that it would have been reduced to no more than a weak idea. This reduction of strength would then have been the only thing which made possible the existence of these unconscious feelings as a separate psychical group.[20]

19. *Studies on Hysteria*, II:86 (my emphasis).
20. *Studies on Hysteria*, II:166–67 (my emphasis).

A quantity of psychical energy that could and should have caused (and found release in) an expression of emotion is instead diverted into causing a physical symptom. So a "quota of emotion" is not itself an emotion, it is a *potential* emotion: that which in the normal course of events *would* cause and find expression in emotion. Freud and Breuer referred to it as "strangulated emotion."[21] When the emotion is too dangerous, however, the potential emotion takes an abnormal course and causes a physical symptom. On occasion Freud says that this process of conversion robs the dangerous idea of its emotion, and, loosely speaking, this is true: for even when the dangerous ideas first reemerge in therapy they seem to the patient to have little importance.[22] Strictly speaking, however, the idea is not robbed of its emotion, but of its *quota* of emotion: that is, of the energy that would normally cause a strong emotional response.

It is essential to this theory that psychical energy can be redirected. A strongly charged incompatible idea can be robbed of its emotion, "*but the sum of excitation which has been detached from it must be put to another use.*"[23] Not only can a quota of emotion—that is, that which would normally cause emotions—be channeled into causing physical symptoms, it can be channeled into causing emotions about inappropriate objects. Even at this early stage in the development of psychoanalysis, Freud recognized that a patient may transfer an emotion that would have been appropriate in a previous situation onto the analyst:

21. *Studies on Hysteria*, II:17.
22. See, e.g., "The Neuro-Psychoses of Defense," III:48–49, and cp. *Studies on Hysteria*, II:285.
23. "The Neuro-Psychoses of Defense," III:48–49 (Freud's emphasis).

Transference onto the physician takes place through a *false connection*. I must give an example of this. In one of my patients the origin of a particular hysterical symptom lay in a wish, which she had had many years earlier and had at once relegated to the unconscious, that the man she was talking to at the time might boldly take the initiative and give her a kiss. On one occasion, at the end of a session, a similar wish came up in her about me. She was horrified at it. . . . What had happened therefore was this. The content of the wish had appeared first of all in the patient's consciousness without any memories of the surrounding circumstances which would have assigned it to a past time. This wish which was present was then, owing to the compulsion to associate which was dominant in her consciousness, linked to my person, with which the patient was legitimately concerned; and as the result of this *mésalliance*—which I describe as a "false connection"—the same emotion was provoked which had forced the patient long before to repudiate this forbidden wish.[24]

For Freud, the irrationality lay, not in the emotion itself, but in the fact that the emotion was directed onto the wrong person. Similarly with phobias: the fear that is manifested in, say, fear of going outside because one might have to urinate is not itself without rationale. The fear appears unjustified and incomprehensible because it has been diverted away from its true object—e.g., a sexual desire for someone which arose contemporaneously with an urge to urinate.[25] Although the sudden need to urinate in a public place may

---

24. See, e.g., *Studies on Hysteria*, II:302–3.
25. E.g., "The Neuro-Psychoses of Defense," III:52–57. Cp. *Studies on Hysteria*, II:293.

be "dangerous," it is more safely dangerous than sexual desire.

The point of catharsis was to redirect the psychical energy back onto its appropriate object.[26]

> The distribution of excitation thus brought about in hysteria usually turns out to be an unstable one. The excitation which is forced into a wrong channel (into somatic innervation) now and then finds its way back to the idea from which it has been detached. . . . The operation of Breuer's cathartic method lies in leading back the excitation in this way from the somatic to the psychical sphere deliberately, and in then forcibly bringing about a settlement of the contradiction by means of thought-activity and a discharge of the excitation by talking.[27]

II

Freud, as we have seen, was not yet in a position to see that it is a mistake to try to explain the conversion of the mental into the physical. For he did not yet understand that the physical symptom was itself a manifestation of archaic mental functioning. The task, then, is not to explain the conversion of a mental process into a physical symptom, but rather to explain the lack of development of a primitive mode

---

26. See, e.g., "The Neuro-Psychoses of Defense," III:49–50; *Studies on Hysteria*, II:124, 283, 296.

27. "The Neuro-Psychoses of Defense," III:50. Cf. also *Studies on Hysteria*, II:283: ". . . the patient only gets free from the hysterical symptom by reproducing the pathogenic impressions that caused it and by giving utterance to them with an expression of emotion, and thus the therapeutic task consists solely in inducing him to do so; when once this task has been accomplished there is nothing left for the physician to correct or remove."

of mental functioning into a conscious, more recognizably mental, expression.

There was, however, a problem with the theory of catharsis that Freud was in a position to see but didn't. Why don't hysterical symptoms naturally tend to die out? Hysterical symptoms are supposedly generated by damming up psychical energy which is then channeled into causing a somatic symptom. But the production and maintenance of a somatic symptom must itself require the expenditure of a certain amount of energy. Since blocking the appropriate emotional response to a traumatic event only involves damming up a finite quantity of energy, this energy should eventually be discharged in the course of producing and maintaining a somatic symptom. Of course, Freud is on his way to discovering the id, or the it, a reservoir of psychic energy, and to formulating a dynamic account of psychic conflict which can explain the maintenance of a somatic symptom. By contrast, the theory of catharsis, which tries to explain both emotions and symptoms in the purely quantitative terms of discharge of energy, cannot account for the stability of a symptom.[28]

But the coup de grace for the theory of catharsis lies in its claim that the dammed-up psychical energy can be used to produce an emotional reaction of similar or increased intensity directed onto an inappropriate object. Phobic reactions and transference phenomena, though emotional and

28. One might try to shore up the theory by arguing that a great reservoir of energy is involved in the expression of an emotion and only a relatively slight amount of energy is involved in the production of a somatic symptom. This strategy does seem ad hoc: for if one were not merely trying to save the theory it would appear that certain somatic symptoms at least required great expenditures of energy for their maintenance. Nor will it ultimately help to say that the energy is dammed up by a counter-cathexis, or counter-investment. For we need to know why both sources of energy don't just peter out.

intense, do not have a cathartic effect: they do not ultimately provide relief. Why is it that the truth cures? Why is it that only the *genuine* emotional response directed onto the right object is successful in discharging the pent-up psychic energy? This question cannot be answered in quantitative terms. So long as one continues to think of an emotion as being (or as being produced by) a quantity of displaceable energy, it will remain mysterious why only the appropriate emotional response has a cathartic effect.

What is crucial to Freud's practice of catharsis, as opposed to his theory, is not the discharge of energy, but rather a person's coming to experience his own desires and fears consciously and with appropriate emotional intensity. Indeed, Freud's method has a Socratic quality to it: through a peculiar type of "cross-examination," the patient's own beliefs about his past and his emotional life are elicited, and eventually "refuted"—in the sense that he is shown to have an inadequate conscious understanding of who he is, what has happened to him and how he feels about it. If a person is willing and able to undergo this "refutation," his own soul will lead the analyst and the analysand to the toxic split-off beliefs and emotions. This process is itself therapeutic. Freud and Breuer discovered that a person can obtain relief from hysterical symptoms by honestly experiencing his own emotions.

One might think that it doesn't really matter if Freud's theoretical understanding of his therapeutic technique is inadequate, for, after all, he abandoned the cathartic method at an early stage of his career. In fact, he is busy modifying his technique throughout these early years, learning from his patients how to conduct a therapy, so that by the end of the *Studies* we can recognize an early but distinctively analytic approach.[29] But if we don't know what catharsis is, we do not know what it is he abandoned. Moreover, Freud never called into question his early therapeutic successes. Long after he abandoned the cathartic method, Freud continued to insist on an important legacy: that catharsis showed that hysterical symptoms have meaning, being substitutes for mental acts, and that the uncovering of this unknown meaning is accompanied by the removal of symptoms.[30] If we do not know what catharsis is, we do not know what these therapeutic achievements consisted in.

Once one abandons the idea that catharsis is a discharge of psychic energy, it begins to look as though catharsis is a conscious unification of thought and feeling. To return to the case of Elisabeth von R., her symptoms were removed only after she was able consciously to accept that she was in love with her brother-in-law and to experience the appropriate feelings. The relief that is experienced when one is at last able emotionally to experience one's thoughts—the relief that is so naturally, if mistakenly, conceived as a discharge—suggests that there is a natural satisfaction in overcoming the divorce between thought and appropriate feeling. Certainly, it cannot be the expression of emotion itself that is relieving, as the discharge theory would suggest. For, as we have seen, hysterical phobias and transferences of emotions onto the analyst involve great "discharges" of emotions, albeit onto inappropriate objects, and they do not provide relief. Relief is provided not by the mere expression of feeling, but by the expression of feeling directed onto the right object. And the fact that the unification of thought and feeling in consciousness is therapeutic,

---

29. See, e.g., "The Psychotherapy of Hysteria," II:255–305.
30. "Two Encyclopedia Articles," XVIII:236.

that pathological symptoms tend to disappear, suggests that progress toward unification of thought and feeling is healthy for human beings. Therapy and cure seem to embody a developmental thrust. The task is to understand why this might be so.

III

Freud cannot undertake this task, at least at the level of theory, for he is working with too unsophisticated a conception of the emotions. For an adequate account of the emotions we must go back to Aristotle. He argued that an emotion should be conceived as providing a *framework* through which the world is viewed.

> When people are feeling friendly and placable, they think one sort of thing; when they are feeling angry or hostile, they think either something totally different or the same thing with a different intensity: when they feel friendly to the man who comes before them for judgement, they regard him as having done little wrong, if any; when they feel hostile, they take the opposite view. Again, if they are eager for and have good hopes of a thing that will be pleasant if it happens, they think that it certainly will happen and be good for them: whereas if they are indifferent or annoyed, they do not think so.[31]

It is unsettling for a modern reader to discover that Aristotle's discussion of the emotions occurs in the *Rhetoric*. The

---

31. *Rhetoric*, II.1, 1377b31–1378a5.

Rhetoric is a handbook for orators: its aim is to teach public speakers how to sway a crowd. And that is precisely why he discusses the emotions. If the orator can manipulate the frame through which his audience interprets the world, then the battle of persuasion is virtually won: the audience will then "see the facts" in a particular light. This is what is unsettling. We tend to think of our emotional lives as private and constitutive of who we are, and it is vaguely offensive to see the study of the emotions consigned to the practical study of the manipulation of people. Aristotle, of course, recognizes that many emotions are characterized by typical bodily responses,[32] and that they are often subjectively experienced as feelings, but he gives pride of place to the way in which emotions locate the individual in the world. "The emotions," he says, "are all those feelings that *so change men as to affect their judgments*, and that are *also* attended by pain or pleasure."[33]

Consider, for example, anger:

Anger may be defined as *a desire accompanied by pain, for a conspicuous revenge for a conspicuous slight at the hands of men who have no call to slight oneself or one's friends*. . . . It must be felt because the other has done or intended to do something to him or one of his friends. It must always be attended by a certain pleasure—that which arises from the expectation of revenge. . . . It is also attended by a certain pleasure because the thoughts dwell upon the act of vengeance, and the images then called up cause pleasure, like the images called up in dreams.[34]

---

32. *On the Soul*, I.1, 403a–b.
33. *Rhetoric*, II.1, 1378a21 (my emphasis).
34. *Rhetoric*, II.2, 1378a31 ff. (my emphasis).

Anger, then, is not merely a feeling or a bodily response, it is an *orientation to the world*. The hostility of a little boy toward his father, for example, is constituted by his recognition that the father stands in the way of his oedipal wishes. The boy must have a view of his social position in the family for him to be able to feel the oedipal emotions. Aristotle allows for a certain subjective experience of anger—it is, he says, a peculiar mixture of pain and pleasure—but the "feel" of anger is a feel one can understand only in the context of its typical causes and effects. Anger is caused by a slight and it motivates revenge.[35]

But an emotion does more than orient the individual to the world: it comes packaged with its own *justification*. The little boy is angry *because* his father frustrates his wishes. This "because" provides not only a cause of the hostility; it provides a reason for it.[36] From the perspective of a little

---

35. For recent valuable work on the emotions, see, e.g., Davidson, "Hume's Cognitive Theory of Pride," in *Essays on Actions and Events*; Gordon, *The Structure of the Emotions*; Roberts, "What an Emotion Is: A Sketch"; de Sousa, *The Rationality of Emotion*. A number of psychoanalytic theorists have been working toward an orientation approach to the emotions. See, e.g., Brenner, "On the Nature and Development of Affects: A Unified Theory" and "Affects and Psychic Conflict"; Novey, "A Clinical View of Affect Theory in Psychoanalysis"; Pulver, "Can Affects Be Unconscious?"; Schafer, "The Clinical Analysis of Affects"; Schur, "Affects and Cognition."

36. There remain within the psychoanalytic community analysts who believe that reasons cannot be causes. This is due to a (mistaken) philosophical tradition which held that the domain of reasons must be distinct from the domain of causes—a tradition which worked its way into psychoanalytic thinking via, e.g., Ricouer's *Freud and Philosophy* and Habermas' *Knowledge and Human Interests*. For an antidote to this way of thinking, see Davidson, *Essays on Actions and Events*, especially Essay 1, "Actions, Reasons and Causes," and Essay 11, "Mental Events." It is crucial to understand that a hermeneutic account of human motivation and action may also be causal. It is a peculiarity of Ricouer and Habermas that they try, unsuccessfully, to develop non-causal hermeneutic accounts. These efforts have been effectively criticized by Grunbaum in *The Foundations of Psychoanalysis*, but it is often assumed that Grunbaum's criticisms apply to all hermeneutic accounts. This is not so. Grunbaum's criticisms are *ad hominem* and do not undermine the more general possibility of a causal hermeneutic account of human motivation.

boy there could be no good reason to block his wishes: thus the frustration is, for him, an outrageous slight. An emotion, for Aristotle, is a structure that makes a claim for its own rationality. Although emotions may (or may not) be expressed in bodily responses, in subjective experiences such as feelings and awareness of bodily response, in fantasies of all sorts, the emotion has not reached full development until it is able to express an explanation and justification of its own occurrence. It thus tries to bring the bodily responses, subjective feelings and fantasies under a rationalizing concept. It tries to bring the unconscious orientation to the world to consciousness.

Not all attempts at rationality succeed, but it is important to distinguish two different types of failure. One type of failure is external to the structure of the mind. Since an emotion provides a framework through which the world is viewed, it is possible to see the world in a certain light even though the world does not genuinely ground the way it is being seen. Here the irrationality is manifested in the mind's being insensitive or oversensitive, unresponsive or overresponsive to the world.[37] Another type of irrationality, though, is internal to the mind itself. The mind may not be able to sustain the self-conscious experience of the fully developed emotion because, for example, the beliefs that justify and partially constitute the emotion conflict with other beliefs. The mind, as Freud discovered, may engage in various strategies to avoid confronting this irrationality. The mind may, for instance, keep the beliefs that rationalize the emotion isolated from those contradicting beliefs that would undermine them. Or it may repress the beliefs that

---

37. For example, paranoid fear often represents the world as more threatening than it is. And even in those cases where the world is in fact as threatening as it is represented, the paranoid fear is not simply a response to that danger.

purport to justify the emotion, so that while a person may have certain subjective feelings or experience certain bodily responses, he has no conscious awareness of the beliefs that are causing those reactions. The emotion is thus being kept in a nascent state, prevented from developing into a fully formed structure.[38]

It is only by the end of his career that Freud will be in a position to understand theoretically the truth he has happened upon at the beginning. Emotions are, by their nature, attempts at rational orientation toward the world. Even an archaic expression of emotion is an archaic attempt at rationality. It is the germ from which a rational orientation may grow. Now, this rationality is not exhausted by an inner coherence of belief and feeling: the rationality of an emotion is also manifested in its being directed onto an appropriate object in the world. An emotion, by its nature, attempts to justify itself. And one can expect archaic expressions of emotion to embody archaic attempts at self-justification. Thus there is a satisfying experience of discharge only when the archaic emotion is directed onto (what from the point of view of archaic mind is) the right object. It seems, then, that Freud happened on a developmental thrust within the individual toward a rational orientation to the world. This is the thrust which he would eventually come to recognize as love.[39] One reason it was difficult to recognize this thrust is that Freud was primarily concerned with the treatment of irrationality. But the *ir*rational is not *a*rational: in humans, the irrational is an attempt to be rational. It may be a failed attempt, or it may be an attempt en route to succeeding.

---

38. Now, insofar as the mind is striving to prevent a recognition of its own irrationality, there can be no such thing as the mere unification of feelings and the beliefs that rationalize them. Any such unification must also involve a transformation.

39. See Chapters 5 and 6.

IV

Freud's early theory of the emotions does not allow him to conceive of them as providing a framework through which the world is viewed. Nor can he conceive emotions as constituted by beliefs, attitudes, justifications, motivations that help orient the person to the world. In fact, in Freud's psychoanalytic practice he is constantly relying on just these features of the emotions to make his diagnoses, but it is just these features which he omits from the psychoanalytic theory of the emotions.[40] The value of treating an emotion as being a quantity of energy, the discharge of that quantity or the subjective appreciation of that discharge is that it holds open the possibility of explaining mental life in quantitative terms.[41] And, of course, a quantitative treatment conforms to Freud's scientific image: it allows Freud to believe that he is approaching the subject of his study from an objective, third-personal point of view and that he is providing a mechanistic explanation of the phenomena. The cost of a quantitative treatment, though, is that it prevents him from seeing that what is at issue is an orientation to the world. And he cannot see that this orientation is present at the base level, in the most primitive expressions of the emotions. For even the basic bodily reactions are an archaic expression of this orientation.

In effect, Freud discovered that the hysteric's life is gov-

---

40. At one point Freud cites Darwin as claiming that the expression of the emotions once served a purpose, and thus had a meaning (II:181), and he develops this idea in *Inhibitions, Symptoms and Anxiety* (XX:87–174), but he is never able explicitly to work through to the concept of an emotion as providing an orientation to the world.

41. The early Freud variously treated an emotion as quantity, discharge or subjective experience of discharge of energy.

erned by an emotional orientation toward an *inner* world.
The hysteric is so afraid of his own desires that he represses
them. Repression is a primitive way to "just say no": its aim
is to enable the person to treat these desires as alien to
himself. Freud's practice of catharsis is designed to help the
hysteric adopt a different emotional orientation toward his
inner world. If one is to understand Freud's practice, as
opposed to his theory, of catharsis, it is worthwhile to consider his account of catharsis in the theater.

If, as has been assumed since the time of Aristotle, the
purpose of drama is to arouse "terror and pity" and so
"to purge" the emotions, we can describe the purpose
in rather more detail by saying that it is a question of
opening up sources of pleasure or enjoyment in our
emotional life. . . . The spectator is a person who
experiences too little, who feels that he is a "poor
wretch to whom nothing of importance can happen,"
who has long been obliged to damp down, or rather
displace his ambition to stand in his own person at the
hub of world affairs; he longs to feel and to act and to
arrange things according to his desires—in short, to
be a hero. And the playwright and actor enable him
to do this by allowing him *to identify himself with* a
hero. They spare him something, too. For the spectator
knows quite well that actual heroic conduct such as
this would be impossible for him without pains and
sufferings and acute fears, which would almost cancel
out the enjoyment. He knows, moreover, that he has
only *one* life and that he might perhaps perish even in
a *single* such struggle against adversity. Accordingly,
his enjoyment is based on an illusion; that is to say,
his suffering is mitigated by the certainty that, firstly,

it is someone other than himself who is acting and suffering on the stage and, secondly, that after all it is only a game, which can threaten no damage to his personal security. In these circumstances he can allow himself to be a "great man," to give way without a qualm to such suppressed impulses as a craving for freedom in religious, political, social and sexual matters and to "blow off steam" in every direction.[42]

To be sure, Freud talks of blowing off steam, but what is important is not this description of tragic catharsis but his characterization of the conditions in which it can occur. It is of the essence of Freud's account of the appeal of great literature that we can in some way, dimly, recognize ourselves in it. And yet, it is only because the spectator remains aware of the gulf that separates his own life from that of the dramatic hero that he can enjoy indulging in imaginative identification. It is in this fine balance of sympathy and distance that a catharsis can occur.[43]

It is precisely this balance of proximity and distance which the hysteric lacks. The hysteric is so afraid of his own desires that they must be kept as far away as possible. This is done in part by repressing them, in part by constructing a life that purports to be complete without them. One of the striking features of the case histories is that there is a stage in which the analysis seems to be complete and yet unsatisfying. Consider, for example, the case of Miss

42. "Psychopathic Characters on the Stage," VII:305–6. It is worth noting that Freud's wife's uncle was the influential classical scholar Jacob Bernays, who in his *Zwei Abhandlungen über die aristotelisch Theorie des Dramas* convinced a generation of scholars that by tragic "catharsis" Aristotle meant a purgation of the emotions. In fact, I think he was wrong about Aristotle, and I discuss this in "Katharsis."

43. I discuss Aristotle's use of this fine balance in "Katharsis."

Lucy R., a patient who had lost her sense of smell and was plagued with olfactory sensations of burnt pudding. One of Freud's working hypotheses was that the smell of burnt pudding must have significance: the smell of burnt pudding must have really been in the air at the time of the psychical trauma. But when he discovered the event, it seemed thoroughly unremarkable: she was cooking with the two young girls who were in her charge when a birthday letter arrived for her from her mother. The young girls grabbed it away from her to prevent her from reading it until her birthday. During the ensuing fracas, the forgotten pudding was burned. When asked by Freud why this scene should be agitating to her, she replied that she was moved that the children should be so affectionate toward her. She was, she said, planning to leave her employ because the other staff were not treating her well and she had not received the support from the children's father and grandfather which she thought she deserved.

This seemed to complete the analysis of the patient's subjective sensation of smell. It had turned out in fact to have been an objective sensation originally, and one which was intimately associated with an experience— a little scene—in which opposing emotions had been in conflict with each other: her regret at leaving the children and the slights which were nevertheless urging her to make up her mind to do so. . . .

But I was not satisfied with the explanation thus arrived at. It all sounded highly plausible, but there was something that I missed, some adequate reason why these agitations and this conflict of emotions should have led to hysteria rather than anything else. Why had not the whole thing remained on the level of normal psychical life? In other words, what was the justification for the conversion which occurred? Why did she not always call to mind the scene itself, instead of the associated sensation which she singled out as a symbol of the recollection?[44]

Another working hypothesis for Freud was that hysteria requires something too terrible to allow into consciousness. "The incompatibility between the single idea that is to be repressed and the dominant mass of ideas constituting the ego" must be so great that consciousness cannot tolerate the threatening idea.[45] Thus although the account Miss Lucy R. gave had a superficial plausibility, the very fact that she had a hysterical symptom implied for Freud that her account had to be rejected. Indeed, Freud's principle implies that one should *always* reject a patient's initial account of the circumstances surrounding the acquisition of his symptom.[46] For Freud, a hysteric always has an idea which is too terrible to contemplate. Without the overwhelmingly dangerous idea, there would be no hysteria.

We can also see this hypothesis at work when Freud reaches a similar plateau in the case of Fräulein Elisabeth von R. Fräulein Elisabeth suffered from pains in the legs and had difficulty in walking. The first phase of her analysis consisted in her recounting a series of misfortunes: her father had fallen ill of a pulmonary edema and she nursed him for eighteen months until he died; her mother's health began to deteriorate; her first sister married someone whom Elis-

---

44. *Studies on Hysteria*, II:115–16 (my emphasis).
45. *Studies on Hysteria*, II:116.
46. Of course, if a patient cannot give an account or can only give an account with obvious lacunae, the analyst can simply push to fill out the picture, but when the patient gives an account which looks complete, the analyst must assume that it isn't.

abeth did not like and who moved his family far away, thus increasing her and her mother's isolation; her second sister died at the birth of her second child.

> As far as the physician was concerned, the patient's confession was at first sight a great disappointment. It was a case history made up of commonplace emotional upheavals, and there was nothing about it to explain why it was particularly from hysteria she fell ill or why her hysteria took the particular form of a painful abasia. It threw light neither on the causes nor the specific determination of her hysteria. We might perhaps suppose that the patient had formed an association between her painful mental impressions and the bodily pains which she happened to be experiencing at the same time, and that now, in her life of memories, she was using her physical feelings as a symbol of her mental ones. But it remained unexplained what her motives might have been for making a substitution of this kind and at what moment it had taken place. These, incidentally, were not the kind of questions that physicians were in the habit of raising. . . . If I had stopped the patient's psychical treatment at this stage, the case of Fräulein Elisabeth von R. would clearly have thrown no light on the theory of hysteria. But I continued my analysis because I firmly expected that deeper levels of her consciousness would yield an understanding both of the causes and the specific determinants of the hysterical symptoms.[47]

In each case, the treatment consisted in bringing the terrible idea into consciousness. Freud and Breuer repeatedly insist

---

47. *Studies on Hysteria*, II:144–45.

that therapeutic success depends on bringing forth the repressed idea with its appropriate emotion. It is this fact
which encouraged them to conceive of catharsis as a discharge of the emotions, and it suggested to us that catharsis
might be a unification of thought and feeling. But for this
to be possible, the terribleness of the terrible idea must be
diminished. Freud must transform the relation between the
terrible idea and "the dominant mass of ideas constituting
the ego" so that the incompatibility between it and the
repressed idea is no longer overwhelming.

In effect, Freud enables the hysteric to transform his
emotional stance toward his own desires. Instead of being
so threatened by them that he must repress them, he becomes able to accept his emotions and thus to allow them
into consciousness. Emotional acceptance and conscious
awareness are of a piece. Since emotions are in part orientations, a change in emotions toward one's desires requires
a change in orientation toward them. Freud encourages his
patients to abandon a hysterical position with respect to the
terrible idea and take up a position of sympathy and distance
reminiscent of the engaged spectator in the theater. He can
now view the traumatic events in his life and experience
the desires, feelings, emotions which would have accompanied those events had they not been too shameful or
threatening to experience. He can also experience some of
the shame or fear involved in having those desires and feelings. He can experience them both because he can sym-
pathetically identify with the person he once was—the
hysteric for whom they were overwhelming—and because
he has left that hysterical position behind. Freud's therapeutic practice consists in establishing the delicate balance
of proximity and distance which makes it possible for the

hysteric to experience a vivid, but nevertheless acceptable emotional response. This is what Freud called a "catharsis."

Since this is not the self-conscious understanding that Freud had of his method, one should not expect to find it explicitly described as such. But throughout the text there are hints that Freud is actively encouraging his patients to alter their emotional orientations toward their inner life. This may not be obvious, for Freud presents himself as such a formidable figure that it may at first be difficult to imagine him creating an atmosphere in which it is sufficiently safe for the patient to experience the terrible idea. One can imagine the fright Elisabeth von R. and Lucy R. must have felt when they realized that their doctor was not willing to rest content with their stories, however complete those stories seemed in themselves. And one should not underestimate the sheer force of the pressure, both physical and mental, which Freud exerted on his patients in his effort to extract their unconscious secrets.[48] But one should also recognize that there is something in Freud's dogged pursuit of his quarry that is cause for relief: however terrible their hidden secret, it is not so abnormal that a doctor, who, after all, has nothing to go on but his knowledge of human nature, cannot guess at the general neighborhood in which the repressed memory lies.

In the case of Elisabeth von R., Freud's vital clue came in a fortuitous event that occurred outside the self-contained universe of the therapeutic sessions: in the midst of a session the patient became quite agitated and tried to end the session when she heard what she knew to be her brother-in-law's footsteps and voice.

---

48. See, e.g., *Studies on Hysteria*, II:153–54, 107–11.

My suspicion was strengthened by this and I determined to precipitate the decisive explanation.[49]

Freud clearly directed her attention onto her relation with
her brother-in-law. She must have realized (at some level
of consciousness) that Freud suspected that this was where
the treasure lay buried. After all, they had already discovered the guilt she felt about going out with a young man
on an evening when her father's condition deteriorated, they
had already discovered that the pain in her leg was located
at the spot on which her father had rested his leg—and
Freud still wasn't satisfied! Yet throughout this revival of
forgotten, painful memories, Freud's attitude was one of
steadfast reassurance:

> During this period of "abreaction" the patient's con-
> dition, both physical and mental, made such a striking
> improvement that *I used to say, only half-jokingly, that
> I was taking away a certain amount of her motives for
> pain every time and that when I had cleared them all
> away she would be well.*[50]

It was in describing her relation to her brother-in-law
that she recollected the scene of her late arrival at her sister's
deathbed, and the dreadful thought she had there: "Now
he is free again and I can be his wife."[51] But there is a sense
in which the catharsis, at least as Freud understood it, had
not yet begun. For although she had remembered the traumatic event, she had not yet emotionally "abreacted" it. Here
is Freud's description of what happened:

---

49. *Studies on Hysteria,* II:155.
50. *Studies on Hysteria,* II:148–49 (my emphasis).
51. *Studies on Hysteria,* II:156.

The period that followed, however, was a hard one for the physician. The recovery of this repressed idea had a shattering effect on the poor girl. She cried aloud when I put the situation drily before her with the words: "So for a long time you had been in love with your brother-in-law." She complained at this moment of the most frightful pains, and made one last desperate effort to reject the explanation: it was not true, I had talked her into it, it could not be true, she was incapable of such wickedness, she could never forgive herself for it. It was easy to prove to her that what she herself had told me admitted of no other interpretation. *But it was a long time before my two pieces of consolation— that we are not responsible for our feelings and that her behavior, the fact that she had fallen ill in these circumstances, was sufficient evidence of her moral character— it was a long time before these consolations of mine made any impression on her.*[52]

Clearly, the period of her catharsis was much taken up with Freud reassuring her that her terrible idea was not that terrible.

In order to mitigate the patient's sufferings I had now to proceed along *more than one path.*[53]

Of course, theory dictated that one path be an emotional "abreaction" or catharsis, and so Freud directed her to work through her fond memories and feelings about her brother-in-law. Freud was convinced that this emotional reaction did her good, *"but I was able to relieve her still more by taking a friendly interest in her present circumstances."*[54] He dis-

---

52. *Studies on Hysteria*, II:157 (my emphasis).
53. *Studies on Hysteria*, II:157 (my emphasis).
54. *Studies on Hysteria*, II:158 (my emphasis).

covered that a slur against the brother-in-law was without foundation and "had the satisfaction of benefiting her by giving her the explanation," he discussed with her the uncertainty of her future prospects: in brief, he made it evident that her terrible idea was, in his judgment, not that terrible. Is it too strong to say that he offered her a (perhaps peculiar) loving reassurance about her inner life?

Freud even drops a hint that the emotional "abreaction" was not the crucial part of the treatment:

> We both had a feeling that we had come to a finish, *though I told myself that the abreaction of the love she had so long kept down had not been carried out very fully.* I regarded her as cured . . .[55]

The fact is that Freud recognized that he had carried out a cathartic cure, even though there had been minimal emotional "abreaction." This did not, however, lead him to rethink what the practice of catharsis consisted in.[56] A sim-

---

55. *Studies on Hysteria*, II:159 (my emphasis).

56. Though there is some evidence that he did not fully accept the model of catharsis as discharge. In "The Psychotherapy of Hysteria," he draws important disanalogies between his therapeutic technique and traditional medical catharsis. A pathogenic idea, he says, is not just like a foreign body, and treatment does not consist in extirpating something. Rather, treatment consists "in causing the resistance [which is responsible for splitting off the pathogenic idea from consciousness] to melt and in thus enabling the circulation to make its way into a region that has hitherto been cut off" (II:290–91). This sounds more like a description of catharsis as making the unconscious conscious rather than catharsis as discharge. (See also II:124, where Freud gives a similar description of the therapeutic process in his account of Miss Lucy R.) There is, moreover, some evidence that Freud's unconscious was at work. In his famous dream of Irma's injection (which occurred on the night of July 23–24, 1895), he has a "Dr. M." making the patently absurd claim of the infected Irma: "There's no doubt it's an infection, but no matter; dysentery will supervene and the toxin will be eliminated" (*The Interpretation of Dreams*, IV:107, 111–12). Dr. M. turns out upon analysis to be Breuer, and while Freud sees that he is making fun of him, treating him as an absurd figure, he doesn't mention that Dr. M's absurd diagnosis bears a striking similarity to Breuer's cathartic method. Isn't catharsis an emotional form of dysentery—an expulsion of the not-well-formed emotions?

ilar oddity was there for Freud to notice in his treatment of Miss Lucy R. Having decided that the story she gave must be inadequate, Freud reasoned:

> If her fondness for the children and her sensitiveness on the subject of the other members of the household were taken together, only one conclusion could be reached. I was bold enough to inform my patient of this interpretation. I said to her: "I cannot think that these are all the reasons for your feelings about the children. I believe that really you are in love with your employer, the Director, though perhaps without being aware of it yourself and that you have a secret hope of taking their mother's place in actual fact. And then we must remember the sensitiveness you now feel towards the servants, after having lived with them peacefully for years. You're afraid of their having some inkling of your hopes and making fun of you."
>
> She answered *in her usual laconic fashion*: "Yes, I think that's true." — "But if you knew you loved your employer why didn't you tell me?" — "I didn't know— or rather I didn't want to know. I wanted to drive it out of my head and not think of it again; and I believe latterly I have succeeded."[57]

Freud thought that this was the best description he had heard "of the strange state of mind in which one knows and does not know a thing at the same time."[58] Now what should have been puzzling to Freud is that Miss Lucy R. showed no emotional reaction to the discovery of her unconscious secret. Yet Freud displays no such puzzlement:

---

57. *Studies on Hysteria*, II:117 (my emphasis).
58. *Studies on Hysteria*, II:117 n.

I expected that this discussion would bring about a fundamental change in her condition. But for the time being this did not occur.[59]

Freud might have thought that therapeutic success did not occur precisely because there was no emotional reaction, but it doesn't seem that he did. He assumed instead that the analysis was not complete. Freud continued the analysis and deeper-seated memories came to the surface: most importantly, of the Director yelling at Miss Lucy R. for allowing another guest to kiss the children. This last scene was the one which had originally dashed her hopes.

After this last analysis, when two days later, Miss Lucy visited me once more, I could not help asking her what had happened to make her so happy. She was as though transfigured. She was smiling and carried her head high. I thought for a moment that after all I had been wrong about the situation, and that the children's governess had become the Director's fiancée. But she dispelled my notion. "Nothing has happened. It's just that you don't know me. You have only seen me ill and depressed. I'm always cheerful as a rule. When I woke yesterday morning the weight was no longer on my mind and since then I have felt well."[60]

There is in this case history no account of an emotional abreaction. The patient and analyst together work through to the traumatic memory and at the next session the patient

59. *Studies on Hysteria*, II:118.
60. *Studies on Hysteria*, II:121.

is cured. If Freud's practice of catharsis really had been one of emotional discharge, the case of Miss Lucy R. should have been puzzling to him. Freud seems not to have noticed that Miss Lucy R. did not have an emotional discharge. The change which does occur in the therapy is in the emotional relation she stands to her own desires and emotions. She began the therapy with a desire and a love that was too terrible to contemplate; she ended the therapy with a love that she could acknowledge consciously and accept.

"And what do you think of your prospects in the house?" — "I am quite clear on the subject. I know I have none, and I shan't make myself unhappy over it." . . . "And are you still in love with your employer?" — "Yes, I certainly am, but that makes no difference. After all, I can have thoughts and feelings to myself."[61]

V

The emotional transformation inherent in catharsis is intimately bound up with the type of responsibility one takes for one's own emotions. Freud consoles Elisabeth von R. by telling her that she is not responsible for her feelings.[62] That is, she should not hold herself responsible in the sense of blaming herself for having fallen in love with her brother-in-law. The attitude of *holding someone responsible* is one that one can take toward oneself or others. In holding oneself responsible one is essentially taking a third-personal stance with respect to oneself and deciding whether one's char-

---

61. *Studies on Hysteria*, II:121.
62. *Studies on Hysteria*, II:157.

acter, actions, thoughts or feelings are worthy of praise or
blame. It is because she would have held herself responsible,
blamed herself, for her love, that Elisabeth von R. archaically denied responsibility via repression. But as she is able
to cease *holding* herself responsible for her emotions, she is
able to *accept* responsibility for them: that is, she is able to
acknowledge them as hers. Accepting responsibility is essentially a first-person relation. In accepting responsibility
I acknowledge who or what I am.[63]

This is something a hysteric cannot do. Suppose a hysteric were to proclaim, "I accept responsibility for my unconscious emotions!" Such a proclamation is just one more
hysterical gesture. The hysteric's conscious and unconscious
stand in too discordant and antagonistic a relation for him
to be able to accept responsibility. The hysteric is tyrannized
not by his unconscious desire, but by his values which treat
the desire as unacceptable. The hysteric speaks from the
position of his values or the false self which takes itself to
be constituted by those values. And hysteria is in its essence
a disclaimer of responsibility for the unconscious. That is
why it makes no sense for the hysteric to accept responsibility for his unconscious. By the very fact that he is a
hysteric, the best he can do is to simultaneously accept and

---

63. That is, accepting responsibility is not essentially a superego, or super-I,
phenomenon. It is holding oneself responsible that is by its nature a superego
activity. The activity of accepting responsibility is only beginning to be understood
by psychoanalysis. Ironically, once one has accepted responsibility for an emotion,
one can, if one wishes, hold oneself responsible for it. Once I accept the emotion
as mine, I can ask: is this the way I want to be? And I can hold myself responsible
for the answer because, in the process of transformation, I have acquired some
ability to shape and control my emotional outlook. By contrast, a hysteric cannot
even raise this question in an intelligible form, in part because the hysteric's mind
has not yet recognized its own functioning. From a hysterical perspective, the
question can only be framed as "Do I want to be paralyzed?" etc. So the hysteric
not only misunderstands the question at issue; he cannot truthfully answer the
question he can pose, for he remains unaware that, say, his paralysis is, for him,
serving a useful purpose. I shall discuss these issues in Chapter 6.

disclaim responsibility: and such an act makes no sense.[64]

Accepting responsibility, then, is not an act of will.[65] And yet, though Freud tells Elisabeth she is not to blame, he also accuses hysterics of "moral cowardice":[66]

> Often enough we have to admit that fending off increasing excitations by the generation of hysteria is, in the circumstances, the most expedient thing to do; more frequently, of course, we shall conclude that a greater amount of moral courage would have been of advantage to the person concerned.[67]

At first glance, this seems all wrong. The issue isn't one of morality—if anything, these patients are suffering from an excess, not a deficiency, of morality—nor does it seem to be one of courage. How could one summon up one's courage for a "choice" that was never under one's conscious control? And yet there is a sense in which courage is at issue. For the task is not simply to face up to the terrible idea. Courage also requires an ability to view it from the right perspective.[68] Courage is a matter of judgment as well as of fearlessness. The hysteric lacks both. A significant part of

64. This is, it is important to note, a significantly different claim from the claim that one cannot simultaneously identify with both the persecuting and the victim fragments of the self. It does seem that one can come to be in a position where one might legitimately say: I am persecuting myself. But the very fact that one can say this is testimony to one's having already left the hysterical position. Although the self may remain divided, so that one can truly recognize persecuting and persecuted fragments, the fact that one is in a position to recognize this, rather than simply be crippled by an alien force, means that one is leaving hysteria behind.

65. This is what most self-help books ignore. Nor is one an absolute authority on whether or not one has accepted responsibility.

66. *Studies on Hysteria*, II:123.

67. *Studies on Hysteria*, II:123.

68. This idea goes back to Socrates, but is elaborated in depth by Aristotle in his account of the virtues or excellences in the *Nicomachean Ethics*.

Freud's early treatments consisted in helping his patients achieve a proper perspective on their repressed desires.

This transformation of one's orientation to a repressed emotion is often facilitated by a reenactment of it. It is this mimetic aspect to the reorientation that Freud took to be a discharge. In fact, it seems that the emotion needs to be rippling archaically through the person if he is to grasp it consciously. The reenactment seems to be needed for the hitherto repressed emotion to complete its process of development: to move from archaic expression toward acquiring the concept with which it can be understood. Here it is not just that a distinctly existing emotion can finally be understood; the understanding helps to constitute the emotion. The conceptualization of an emotion is a development within the emotion itself. It is this development that allows one to transform one's relationship to it.

But what is this transformation? If one thinks of this question in its broadest context—as asking what is being transformed, who or what is doing the transforming and what the activity of transformation is—then one can read most of the subsequent unfolding of Freudian psychoanalysis as an attempt to answer it. For psychoanalysis unfolded much as an analysand's self-understanding unfolds in the course of an analysis. In fact, it was in trying to understand the analysand's transformation that psychoanalysis was itself transformed. And what Freud grasped by the end of his career, if dimly, is that both transformations, in the individual and in psychoanalysis, were manifestations at different levels of the very same process.

3

The Interpretation
of Dreams

I

In dreams Freud recognized what has all along been before
our eyes: archaic mind. *The Interpretation of Dreams* begins
with the following remarkable claim:

> In the pages that follow I shall bring forward proof
> that there is a psychological technique which makes
> it possible to interpret dreams, and that, if that pro-
> cedure is employed, *every dream reveals itself as a
> psychical structure which has a meaning and which can
> be inserted at an assignable point in the mental activities
> of waking life.*[1]

Freud is, in effect, extending the domain in which the mind
can see itself at work. Nothing less is at stake than mind's
ability to comprehend its relation to reality. By the end of
the nineteenth century, Freud realized that, for all his me-
chanical models, he did not understand how the mind

---

1. *The Interpretation of Dreams*, IV:1 (my emphasis).

worked. In his early work with hysterics, he assumed his patients were dredging up memories of traumatic experiences. The mind's relation to reality was more or less taken for granted. It was a passive recipient of experience: a wax tablet that received and held the impress of reality. But, as is by now well known, Freud came to doubt that all his patients' reports and his own self-analysis could be a simple reflection of the past.[2] He found it incredible that all the repeated accounts of childhood seduction, "*not excluding my own*," could be straightforward memories. It is misleading to say that Freud abandoned belief in the sexual abuse of children: to the end of his career he was convinced that actual sexual abuse contributed to the development of neurosis in later life.[3] Freud's discovery depends only on the alleged memories of abuse not being always and everywhere what they purport to be. Mind, then, must be active in its presentation of the past.

With the discovery of the mind's activity, Freud must have realized that he had little idea of what the unconscious is like. If hysterics are not suffering from "reminiscences," there must be something else in the unconscious from which they are suffering. And if mind is active in organizing "experience," what is it doing? No wonder Freud considered *The Interpretation of Dreams* to be his greatest book. For it is here that Freud begins to understand what is in the unconscious and how it works.

Freud would not have been able to understand the bizarre workings of the mind if he were not able to see some rationality hidden in them. Freud began with dreams, and his claim for their rationality is encapsulated in the thesis

---

2. See the letter to Fliess of September 21, 1897, in *The Complete Letters of Sigmund Freud to Wilhelm Fliess*, 1887–1904.
3. See, e.g., *An Outline of Psycho-Analysis* (1938), XXIII:187.

that every dream has a meaning. Indeed, it is by deciphering the meaning of a dream that Freud at once makes a claim for its intelligibility and reveals the contents of the unconscious. Psychoanalysis tends to move simultaneously in two directions. On the one hand, it tries to discover a hidden irrationality in the thought, speech and action which presents itself as rational. On the other hand, it tries to find rationality hidden within the irrational. There among the flotsam of dreams, physical symptoms, slips of the tongue, psychoanalysis discovers that mind is active.

But what is it for a dream to have meaning? Freud says that dreams are *psychical acts*.[4] I would like to take up this idea and suggest that dreams are like actions.[5] Now, action

---

4. *The Interpretation of Dreams*, V:533
5. It is often thought that the meaning of a dream is like the meaning of language. And it is true, as Freud realized, that the fundamental item of interpretation is not the dream itself, but the analysand's report of the dream; and this does occur in a structured, communicative situation (V:512, 611). Nevertheless, language does not provide the right model of meaning. Language is in its essence an instrument of communication. Linguistic expressions do not have meaning in themselves; they gain their meaning through the shared and recognized intentions of speakers to use these expressions to communicate with each other. (Grice, "Meaning"; Davidson, "Radical Interpretation," in *Inquiries into Truth and Interpretation*; Wittgenstein, *Philosophical Investigations*, I.80–242.) This communicative intention seems to be absent from dreams. Dreams, Freud cautioned, "are not made with the intention of being understood" (V:341). (In contrasting dreams with jokes, Freud also says: "A dream is a completely asocial mental product; it has nothing to communicate to anyone else . . . ," *Jokes and Their Relation to the Unconscious*, VIII:179.) Linguistic meaning also seems to depend essentially on the practical commitment of speakers to adhere to public norms. If someone tells his doctor, say, that he fears his arthritis is spreading to his thigh, he must be willing to accept the doctor's correction that arthritis is not a disease that can spread to the thigh (Burge, "Individualism and the Mental"). He may of course make a mistake about the meaning of "arthritis," but if he remains unwilling to accept an expert's correction on the use of the term, we start to lose grip on the idea that by his use of "arthritis" he means arthritis. Suppose now that someone tells his analyst that he dreamt arthritis spread to his thigh. There is no similar basis for correction. It would be a mistake for the analyst to say, "You couldn't have dreamt that arthritis spread to your thigh, you must have dreamt that something that *felt like* arthritis had spread to your thigh." The analysand need have dreamt no such thing. The dream arthritis might not have felt like arthritis. All the analysand is sure of is that it was *arthritis*. We cannot begin to capture the

is by its nature meaningful. Every action is an attempt to satisfy an agent's desire, under the constraints of an agent's beliefs about the world. To take a boring example: if I want another sip of the lukewarm coffee I've been drinking, and I believe that the cup is just to my right, then—given that I don't have a stronger desire to finish this sentence, etc.— my right hand will pick up the cup and bring it to my lips. It is precisely because we can see this action as an attempt to satisfy a desire, given certain beliefs, that we can see it as meaningful. And it is precisely this feature that makes us see the action *as an action*, rather than as a mere twitch or meaningless motion.

Of course, there are differences between dreams and actions. For one thing, a person's beliefs play a crucial role in the formation of an action, while in dreams this does not seem to be so. We dream we can fly, that we are talking to a dead relative, that some impossible romance is being consummated. In dreams, beliefs seem to take the night off. And yet, this is not a crucial difference. One might think of a dream as the act of an omnipotent being. Suppose there is no way the world is, independent of this being's judgment of how he wanted it to be. Then not only would it not be necessary for him to consult his beliefs about the world before acting; there would be no point in his doing so. The reason we non-omnipotent beings take belief into account is that the world is not immediately, magically submissive to our wills. If we want to satisfy our desires, we must consider the best way to satisfy them given the way the

surface of this dream, the "manifest content," if we assume from the outset that the dreamer could not possibly mean what he appears to be saying. Thus a dream's meaning does not seem to bear the same responsiveness to public norms ordinarily embodied in linguistic use. This gives us reason to think that the unconscious cannot be "structured like a language." (Cp. Lacan, e.g., "The Function and Field of Speech and Language in Psychoanalysis," in *Ecrits*.)

world is. But if as dreamers we "act" as though we were omnipotent beings, belief is irrelevant. Wishing makes it so!

In fact, beliefs do help to shape a dream. According to Freud, it is only childhood dreams that are the direct expressions of a wish.[6] In adults, dreams are the joint product of two opposing forces, infantile wishes that are striving to obtain satisfaction and censoring forces.[7] Just as an action is the attempt to satisfy desire under the constraint of belief, so a dream is the attempt to gratify a wish under the constraint of censorship. And the censoring faculty must be sensitive to the dreamer's beliefs, hopes and values. For the point of censorship is to prevent the agent from recognizing the conflict between his adult outlook and the infantile wish striving for gratification. If the censoring faculty were insensitive to this outlook, there would be no basis for censoring the dream one way rather than another.

Freud thinks that there is a continuity between dreaming and waking life. A dreamer remains sensitive to external stimuli: he will, for example, readily weave a noise in his environment into his dream. Freud speculates that here the desire to continue sleeping aids the infantile wish. In fact, when the content of a dream becomes threatening, the dreamer may often reassure himself that he is only dreaming. "I am driven to conclude," Freud says, "that *throughout our whole sleeping state we know just as certainly that we are dreaming as we know that we are sleeping.*"[8] So while there is a sense in which our dreams are marvelously free of our waking beliefs, there is another sense in which our mind is

6. See *The Interpretation of Dreams*, IV: Chapter 3, esp. p. 127.
7. See, e.g., *The Interpretation of Dreams*, IV:144.
8. *The Interpretation of Dreams*, V:571. See also *Jokes and Their Relation to the Unconscious*, VIII:165.

all along keeping track of the fact that we are dreaming and of how our emerging dream might conflict with our conscious, waking self. The dream, then, is like an action: it is an attempted gratification of a wish under the constraint of certain sorts of beliefs.[9]

---

9. Another suggestion is that a dream's meaning be understood as the natural relation of a symptom to its underlying cause (Shope, "Freud's Concepts of Meaning"). Just as spots signify measles, so the remembered dream is the conscious effect of an unconscious wish which is its meaning. One virtue of this suggestion is that it does not require dreams to embody any communicative intentions. Nor need there be any adherence to public norms. The measles in a young child is not trying to make itself known; nor is it striving to behave in this child as it does in other children. All that is required is that there be a regular relation between an apparent effect and a non-apparent underlying cause. Nevertheless, a dream seems to be much too rich a phenomenon for its meaning to be fully captured by the natural relation between symptom and underlying cause. In cases of natural meaning, there is a direct and virtually invariable relation: a certain type of spot on the skin is a sign of measles because its presence is regularly correlated with the presence of measles. There is no such direct relation between the remembered dream and the unconscious wish which is its cause. A critical mistake in previous attempts to interpret dreams, according to Freud, is the assumption that there is a fixed key for decoding the message of a dream (IV:96–105). There is no direct or invariable relation between the elements in the remembered dream and the underlying wish, so any attempt at decoding must fail. As Freud said, "the same piece of content may conceal a different meaning when it occurs in various people or various contexts" (IV:105). (See also V:471, where Freud says that every element in a dream can, for purposes of interpretation, stand for its opposite just as easily as for itself. Only within the full context of the dreamer's life—the outward events of his life and his inward wishes, hopes and fears—can one decide. Cp. IV:318.) To understand the meaning of a remembered dream, Freud insists that one must look both *outward* to the environment in which the person is situated and *"inward"* to the wishes, hopes and fears of the person whose dream it is. For the dream is constructed from material taken from recent waking experience, but is also related to an unconscious wish which motivates the dream (IV:181). One needs to understand how the dream stands at the junction between a person's inner and outer life to understand its meaning. (For an example of this, see Freud's analysis of his dream of the botanical monograph, IV:169–76.) A natural sign does not stand in such a complex and variable relation to its cause.

II

But what is a wish? It is often assumed that a wish is just a desire, but that cannot be right.[10] The concept of desire is that of a motivating force which, jointly with belief, produces action.[11] There is no way into the concept of desire other than by the way it works in conjunction with belief to produce action.[12] A wish occupies a different role. Like desire, a wish is a motivating force, but, unlike desire, its products are not actions. Dreams are *like* actions; they aren't actions. A wish works within a different, archaic form of mental functioning. Just as one only discovers what a desire is by capturing its role within the relatively advanced form of mental activity that leads to action, so one can only discover what a wish is via its role within the archaic activity in which it finds its home. It is a mistake to think that an infantile wish is just the desire of an infant. That is to treat

10. French translators use *désir* as a translation for the German *Wunsch* (which is accurately translated into English as "wish," not "desire"). Because the French refrained from using *vœu*, which accurately translates *Wunsch*, it would be difficult for them even to formulate the problem I am going to pose. (Similarly, the Italian translation is *desiderio*; the Spanish is *deseo*.)

11. Indeed, desire and belief are characterized by the way they jointly determine rational action: To *desire that ø* is to be disposed to act in ways that would tend to bring it about that ø in a world in which one's beliefs, whatever they are, were true. To *believe that ø* is to be disposed to act in ways that would satisfy one's desires, whatever they are, in a world in which ø (together with one's other beliefs) were true. Therefore, desires are not detectable in isolation: they are isolated as the motivation element in the overall interpretation of a person who is able to act on the basis of his beliefs and desires. See Stalnaker, *Inquiry*, p. 15; Davidson, "Radical Interpretation," in *Inquiries into Truth and Interpretation.*

12. This is the so-called holism of the mental. For a good introduction to holism and its relation to psychoanalysis, see Hopkins' "Introduction" in *Philosophical Essays on Freud* (Wollheim and Hopkins, eds.). For evidence that Freud himself believed in the holism of the mental, see *The Interpretation of Dreams*, V:511: "No conclusions upon the construction and working methods of the mental instrument can be arrived at or at least fully proved from even the most painstaking investigation of dreams or of any other mental function taken *in isolation*."

the infant as a homunculus: a little person, differing from the adult mainly in size. The infantile wish is a motivating force within the infant, to be sure, and it may well be an ancestor of desire, but we do not do justice to the evolution of an individual mind if we treat the ancestor as merely an instance of its descendant.

Freud implicitly recognizes that a wish differs from a desire. For he characterizes a wish by its role within the archaic functioning of the infantile mind.[13] Freud discovered a type of mental activity that differs so dramatically in form from conceptual thinking that, as I have said, it is one of Freud's greatest achievements simply to recognize it as mental. He called this archaic activity "*primary process*" to signify that it was the earliest form of mental functioning. Freud called the conceptual thinking with which we are familiar "*secondary process*." Secondary-process thinking, Freud thought, developed out of the archaic, primary-process mental functioning. Primary-process mental activity tends to be expressed in concrete images, rather than in concepts, and it tends to proceed by loose associations.[14] That is, from the point of view of the secondary-process mind that is trying to understand it, primary process seems to slip along a path of superficial similarities. And primary process pays no respect to logic. "Thoughts which are mutually contradictory make no attempt to do away with each other," Freud says, "but persist side by side."[15] This cannot be quite right because a primary-process "thought" is so called as a matter of courtesy: it does not exist in conceptualized form. Freud's point is, for example, that a child's love for a parent may exist in the unconscious alongside his hatred for the very

---

13. See *The Interpretation of Dreams*, V:565 ff., 597–601.
14. See, e.g., *The Interpretation of Dreams*, V:595–97.
15. *The Interpretation of Dreams*, V:596.

same parent, and that neither emotion will diminish the force of the other. Indeed, both emotions may be represented in the same dream image of devouring the parent. In the same act the parent is ingested, protected, kept close, and is also destroyed.[16]

The outcome of primary-process activity is not an action designed to satisfy the wish, but a concrete, imagistic representation of the conditions that would satisfy it.[17] In the case of an adult's dream, this is not obvious, because the infantile wish causing the dream is repressed. If the dream is to escape a similar fate, it must provide a disguised satisfaction.[18] Freud hypothesizes that this primary-process activity occurs, without repression, in infancy. The primal mental activity occurs at the breast. The infant forms an image of conditions in which his hunger is satisfied and the next time he feels those inner stirrings, he hallucinates that image.[19] If one were looking at this mental activity solely from the developmental perspective of how an individual comes to perceive and relate to his environment, one would be impressed how similar it is to the reality-based thinking of adult life. Indeed, from a developmental perspective, it looks as though infantile mental life is en route toward a more mature appreciation of the world. After all, the infant has already learned that feeding at the breast satisfies its hunger, and it is able to form a wish for the breast. From this perspective, *the hallucination is an integral part of the wish itself*. It is not the satisfaction of a wish so much as an

---

16. This is discussed at length in *Totem and Taboo*, XIII, but see esp. pp. 141–42. And see *Three Essays on the Theory of Sexuality*, VII:222.

17. Our attention is here confined to the phenomenon of dreams. Primary process may, of course, have myriad other manifestations.

18. See, e.g., *The Interpretation of Dreams*, IV:144. (For Freud, only childhood dreams are direct expressions of a wish: IV:127.)

19. See, e.g., *The Interpretation of Dreams*, V:565–66. Cp. "Formulations on the Two Principles of Mental Functioning," XII:219.

expression of the content of the wish. It is what the wish is a wish for.

This is not Freud's perspective. He was investigating archaic thinking from the perspective of someone who wanted to account for the strange phenomenon of the dream. And he worked retrospectively: he began with adult analysands' dream reports, and on that basis constructed an account of infantile mental life. Freud was convinced from his clinical experience that dreams provide a gratification of wishes. They do not merely express them. And he explained dreaming as "a piece of infantile mental life that has been superseded."[20] Since dreaming is an attempt to satisfy an infantile wish, and dreaming is a form of infantile mental life, it is natural to conclude that the infant's hallucinations must be satisfying. After all, the infant could not have a firmly established sense of the difference between a perceptual and a hallucinatory experience. If the perceptual experience is satisfying, it is plausible to suppose that the barely distinguishable hallucinatory experience is also satisfying. And if these hallucinations are satisfying, it is a short step to conclude that the *aim* of a wish is to achieve these "experiences" of satisfaction. Freud took this step. He concluded that primary-process mental activity differs from secondary process not only in form but also in function. The point of archaic mental functioning, for Freud, is not to express the wish's demand, but to satisfy it. The psychical impulse that causes the hallucination to occur, he argues, is the wish. And the hallucination provides an experience of satisfaction. Thus, Freud reasons, the hallucination is the *aim* of this mental activity: "the aim of this first psychical activity was to produce a 'perceptual identity'—a repetition

---

of the perception that was linked with the satisfaction of the need."[21]

This reasoning is plausible. It is also suspect. It depends on assuming that the function of archaic mental life in the infant is essentially the same as it is in the adult dreamer. No room is allowed for the possibility that archaic mental functioning might *acquire a function* that it did not have at the beginning of mental life. And the implications of this assumption are enormous. For if the aim of archaic mental functioning is—right from the beginning—to produce hallucinatory experiences of satisfaction, the archaic mind has to be very different from the adult mind that grows out of it. Indeed, archaic mind must be operating according to its own principle. For, according to Freud, this isn't a primitive attempt to get reality to satisfy the wish; it is, rather, a primitive attempt to provide a hallucinatory satisfaction. Freud is now forced to describe not only two different *levels* of mental activity but two different *principles* of mental functioning.

Unfortunately, Freud rose to the task.[22] The earliest function of the mind, Freud speculated, is simply to discharge tension. This tension is produced by a bodily need, and it, in turn, produces an unpleasurable experience. The paradigm is hunger. A bodily need produces the experience of hunger, and it is uncomfortable to be hungry. Now, the infantile mind, Freud argues, is not yet concerned with getting fed. It just wants to discharge the accumulating tension, and it tries to do so in the quickest possible way. The mind simply produces a hallucination of the breast. That is, it hallucinates the conditions in which bodily need

---

21. *The Interpretation of Dreams*, V:566.
22. See, e.g., *The Interpretation of Dreams*, V:597–602. Cp. "Formulations on the Two Principles of Mental Functioning," XII:218–20.

is satisfied. This provides a path along which the tension can be discharged, and this discharge is experienced as pleasure. The infantile mind, Freud said, operates according to "the pleasure principle": its sole aim is to discharge tension along the shortest possible route. True to his scientific image, Freud characterizes the pleasure principle from a mechanistic point of view.

Of course, this archaic mental activity cannot satisfy bodily needs. A hallucinated breast does not fill a hungry tummy. And so the mind must organize itself according to a different principle of mental functioning. For Freud, frustration is the motor of mental development. Because hallucinations do not ultimately satisfy hunger, the infant must become more attentive to reality. The mind begins to operate according to a different principle. Instead of aiming at immediate discharge of tension, it becomes sensitive to the conditions in reality that would genuinely satisfy the bodily need. The mind begins to work according to "the reality principle." To be able to do this, the mind must be able to inhibit the immediate discharge of tension; it must be able to store memories and redirect energy through the roundabout route of voluntary movement. In this way, a person can learn from, respond to and alter the world so as to obtain genuine satisfaction. According to Freud, primary-process mental activity occurs in a mind that is functioning according to the pleasure principle. The images and loose associations of a dream are all tripping along the fastest route to discharge. Secondary process, by contrast, occurs in a mind functioning according to the reality principle.[23] Conceptual thinking is directed toward obtaining satisfaction from the world.

23. By the time he wrote *Beyond the Pleasure Principle* in 1920, Freud's views had changed. I shall discuss this in Chapters 5 and 6.

Freud should not have so segregated primary from secondary process. For though it is clear from Freud's picture *that* the mind must change its functioning from the pleasure principle to the reality principle, it is mysterious *how* this transition is supposed to occur. The reality principle is portrayed as so unlike the pleasure principle that there is no natural way for the one to develop out of the other. Freud admits that his portrayal of the infantile mind is a "fiction": "an organization which was a slave to the pleasure principle and neglected the reality of the external world could not maintain itself alive for the shortest time, so that it could not have come into existence at all." Nevertheless, he continues, the fiction is justified because the infant is *almost* like this—"*provided one includes with it the care it receives from its mother*"![24] But if, as Freud here suggests, we take the basic unit to be the infant-mother dyad, there is no longer any reason to conceive the infantile mind as operating according to the pleasure principle. A mother in tune with her child will meet his emerging hunger with a real breast. There will be no firm distinction between fantasied and real breast, as hallucinated wish is followed by perceived satisfaction. That is, the hallucination can be conceived as an expression of the wish.

Freud, by contrast, is led by his commitment to the pleasure principle to an implausible conception of the wish. Within his mechanistic model, a wish is just the current that seeks discharge.[25] And, as we have seen, the *aim* of a wish is to produce a hallucination of satisfaction. After all,

---

24. "Formulations on the Two Principles of Mental Functioning," XII:220 n. (my emphasis). See also *The Interpretation of Dreams*, V:598, where he also calls the primitive psychical apparatus a fiction.

25. *The Interpretation of Dreams*, V:598. Its presence in the mind is experienced as unpleasure, it sets in motion the primitive mental mechanism, and the discharge is experienced as pleasure.

the wish is working in a mind operating according to the pleasure principle, and such a mind can have no other goal than the direct discharge of tension through hallucination. But then a wish for the breast turns out to be a desire for a hallucinatory experience of the breast. This is implausible. It is so much more compelling to think of the wish as an archaic form of desire for the real thing, the breast. Freud is forced to characterize it as a full-fledged desire for the wrong thing.

In any case, Freud himself says much to make it implausible that a wish could by its nature be aimed at producing a hallucination. For example, in his first discussion of the Oedipus complex he says:

> If anyone dreams, with every sign of pain, that his father or mother or brother or sister has died, I should never use the dream as evidence that he wishes for that person's death *at the present time*. The theory of dreams does not require as much as that; it is satisfied with the inference that this death has been wished for at some time or other during the dreamer's childhood.[26]

Taken literally, this passage does not make sense. Freud's theory depends on the dreamer having the wish at the time of the dream. For it is the wish that motivates the dream and it is the wish that is satisfied by it. It is the essence of Freud's theory that infantile wishes continue to exist in the adult, albeit unconsciously. Freud is aware of this, and just two paragraphs later he corrects himself:

> Many people . . . who love their brothers and sisters and would feel bereaved if they were to die, harbor

---

26. *The Interpretation of Dreams*, IV:249 (Freud's emphasis). See IV:248–67.

evil wishes against them in their unconscious, dating from earlier times; and these are capable of being realized in dreams.[27]

What Freud seems to be saying, then, is that the adult dreamer does not *desire* the death of his loved one. He does not want this person to die. The infantile wish that lives on in him and motivates his dream must, therefore, be distinguished from a desire. The theory of dreams, Freud says, only requires that the dreamer actually have wished for the death sometime during his childhood. But neither is it plausible to assume that this childhood wish, as it was alive in the breast of the child, was really only aimed at a hallucination. The child wishes for the real thing: that his rival should disappear! Most of the time he has to make do with a fantasy, a sort of consolation prize.

Freud says that the content of a child's wish for the death of a sibling or parent is different from the adult counterpart because the child has no conception of death beyond the absence of his rival.[28]

Thus if a child has reasons for wishing the absence of another, there is nothing to restrain him from giving his wish the form of the other child being dead. And the psychical reaction to dreams containing death-wishes proves that, in spite of the different content of these wishes in the case of children, they are nevertheless in some way or other the same as the wishes expressed in the same terms by adults.[29]

27. *The Interpretation of Dreams*, IV:251.
28. *The Interpretation of Dreams*, IV:254–55.
29. *The Interpretation of Dreams*, IV:255.

Freud's point is that the infantile wish differs in content from what would be the content of the corresponding adult desire. For the desire would have absorbed into its content a richer conception of what it is for a person to be dead. Thus in spite of his theory, Freud distinguishes wish from desire not by their differing aims, but by the inchoate content of the wish. And the horrified reaction of an adult to his dream can be explained as the reaction of the emotional-desiring part of the adult toward the childhood wishes that live on unconsciously in his soul. But while the mature adult does not desire the death of a loved one, even though he continues to harbor an infantile wish, it does not make sense to claim that the horrified reaction is toward a wish aimed at a hallucination. The horrified reaction is toward a wish for the real thing.

III

If we can let go of the "fiction" of the infantile mind operating according to the pleasure principle, we can then see the infant as directed onto the world from the beginning of mental life.[30] This explains, as Freud's story cannot, how the infant has already learned to hallucinate the breast when it is hungry. Of course, there need be no firm distinction for the infant between hallucination and perception, between subjective and objective experience, between self and external world.[31] The point is only that the transition from

---

30. This has the advantage of according with current empirical research. See Stern, *The Interpersonal World of the Infant.*

31. See Winnicott, e.g., "Primitive Emotional Development" and "Transitional Objects and Transitional Phenomena," in *Through Paediatrics to Psycho-Analysis*; "The Theory of the Parent-Infant Relationship," in *The Maturational Process and the Facilitating Environment*; and Loewald, e.g., "Ego and Reality," in *Papers on Psychoanalysis.*

primary to secondary process lies on a developmental continuum of mental functioning. The concrete images of primary process may be *pre*conceptual, but they are also *proto*conceptual. They are *that from which* concepts emerge. And the loose associations of primary process are, it must be remembered, loose only from the perspective of mature conceptual thinking. One might think of the transition from the loose associations of archaic thinking to the tight conceptual links in the following way. The mind is not just gathering facts; it is learning how to think. The loose associations of archaic mind represent the infant's primitive sense of similarity and relevance. This sense of similarity is itself honed and refined, so that by the time a person is able to think conceptually, the associations of primary process appear to him to be loose. Thus, in the development of mind, there is no fundamental transition of principles of mental functioning that needs to be explained. Nor need it be mysterious how the mind can recognize itself in primary-process activity. To be sure, archaic mind puts on a strange face to the secondary-process mind that is trying to understand it. And yet, staring into that face, the mind can eventually come to see that it is looking into a (perhaps distorted) mirror.

It remains to explain the phenomenon of dreams. Freud's clinical experience convinced him that the dream does not merely express a wish; it attempts to gratify it. That is why he was led to posit the pleasure principle as the earliest form of mental functioning. If we are to avoid this "fiction," we need an account of how the dream might acquire the function of gratification in the course of mental development. Ironically, Freud himself provides the materials with which to construct this account. It is implicit in his theory of sexuality. The sexual drive, according to Freud, is by its very nature *detachable*. At the beginning of human life, Freud says, there is nothing observable that would lead one to posit a distinctively sexual drive.[32] The biological functions, like sucking at the mother's breast, may be pleasurable, but that alone would only provide evidence that satisfying bodily needs is pleasurable. Freud posited a class of drives aimed at self-preservation, like hunger. So far, there is only evidence for the self-preservative drives. However, in the course of development, the sexual drive detaches itself from self-preservative activities.[33] The phenomenon that attracted Freud's attention was thumb-sucking. Thumb-sucking is not nourishing, and it does not contribute to self-preservation. Freud thinks that sucking at the breast is so pleasurable for the infant that the need for reexperiencing this sensual pleasure becomes detached from the need for nourishment. Sucking itself becomes pleasurable. It is only when the sexual drive detaches itself from the self-preservative drives in this way that we are able to see it at work.

It is in just this way, I would like to suggest, that hallucinating *becomes* pleasurable. The hallucination of the breast is originally produced as an expression of the content of the wish. It is what the wish is a wish for. But, as we have seen, the infant has no firmly established distinction between hallucination and perception, between fantasy and reality. A good-enough mother, in tune with the baby's emerging needs, will meet his hallucination with a breast.[34] The hallucination will thus be infused with the pleasure of

---

32. *Three Essays on the Theory of Sexuality*, VII:182.

33. *Three Essays on the Theory of Sexuality*, VII:181–82. I shall discuss the significance of detachability in Chapters 5 and 6.

34. Cp. Winnicott, "Ego Distortion in Terms of True and False Self" and "The Theory of the Parent-Infant Relationship," in *The Maturational Process and the Facilitating Environment*.

sucking at the breast. And due to the detachable nature of the sexual drive, the pleasure originally attached to the satisfaction of a natural need becomes attached to the mental representation of this satisfaction. The archaic mind itself becomes sexualized, and thus it is preserved. (If one wants to continue talking of principles of mental functioning, one might thus conclude that the pleasure principle develops out of the reality principle rather than vice versa.)

IV

The interpretation of dreams gave Freud his first deep insight into the contents of the unconscious. What he found there were infantile wishes. He thought that was all he found, and that puzzled him.[35] In fact, Freud discovered more than wishes in the unconscious, but he was not in a position fully to understand his discovery. The essence of repression, Freud says, is the transformation of emotion, but he couldn't grasp this transformation because he was laboring with an inadequate conception of an emotion.[36] Freud conceived of a psychic experience as having two parts. There would be an idea—like "I am in love with my brother-in-law"—and that idea would have a certain charge of psychic energy attached to it. An emotion, for Freud, is the discharge of energy caused by an idea, or the awareness of that discharge.[37] The discharge of energy is typically expressed in bodily functions—for example, in increased pulse, trembling, sweating, blushing, etc. Sometimes Freud identifies the emotion with the processes of motor and secretory

---

35. *The Interpretation of Dreams*, V:565.
36. *The Interpretation of Dreams*, V:604; cp. 606.
37. *The Interpretation of Dreams*, V:581–82; cp. 468, 537 n.

discharges caused by the idea; sometimes he identifies emotions with the awareness of those processes, and in this way identifies emotions with feelings. Either way, the emotion is that which the idea would bring about if it could.

The point of repression, for Freud, is to prevent this causal story from unfolding.[38] The so-called "wishful impulses" are ideas that in infancy would have caused pleasurable emotions, but now, due to their conflict with conscious values and purposes, would cause unpleasurable feelings. These ideas are kept out of consciousness in order to inhibit the generation of this unpleasure. The essence of repression, Freud says, is the transformation of emotion. Now, for Freud, emotions must be conscious. When there is a discharge of energy, there is a typical conscious awareness of that discharge. For example, a person will *feel* his hands trembling, he will *feel* his heart start to pound. Let us use the word "feeling" narrowly, to cover only these conscious feels. Then, roughly speaking, Freud treated emotions as feelings. Either they are feelings or, more strictly, they are processes of discharge which feelings accompany. Either way, we must in some way be aware of an emotion when it is occurring. So Freud thought. And thus Freud, who argued so vigorously that mental life should not be equated with conscious mental life, was, by his own conceptualization, forced to equate emotional life with conscious emotional life.[39] And yet, though there is no place for unconscious emotions in Freud's *theory*, if we conceive of emotions as providing an orientation to the world, we

---

38. See, e.g., *The Interpretation of Dreams*, V:604, 581–82.

39. By 1915, when Freud published "The Unconscious," he explicitly draws this consequence, arguing that, strictly speaking, there cannot be unconscious emotions (XIV:178). Cp. *The Ego and the Id*, XIX:22–23.

can see that *in practice* Freud is constantly relying on unconscious emotions.[40]

Psychoanalysis exists only because repression is unable to carry out its task. An idea, even though repressed, may nevertheless have causal efficacy. It may be able to generate some of the feelings and discharges that would appropriately accompany it. This is what Freud means by saying that emotions are least influenced by censorship.[41] He argues that one cannot deal with the expression of emotion in a dream in the same dismissive fashion as one is accustomed to treating the content: "If I am afraid of robbers in a dream, the robbers, it is true, are imaginary—but the fear is real."[42] The fear is real not just because it is felt. The emotions experienced in dreams seem to make a demand on us to make sense of them: "dreams insist with greater energy on their right to be included among our real mental experiences in respect to their emotional than in respect to their ideational content."[43]

The problem is that it is not obvious how to include them. We do not know how to understand an emotion, Freud says, "unless it is linked to a piece of ideational material"—that is, unless it is accompanied by beliefs that rationalize it.[44] Freud thus comes to the brink of recognizing that an emotion is an orientation to the world constituted

40. What is crucial to an emotion is the orientation it provides, and this may be unconscious. An emotion may characteristically be infused with certain bodily responses, subjective awareness of these responses and feelings. And when they occur they partially constitute the emotion; they are not just concomitants. But these characteristics are neither necessary nor sufficient for the presence of an emotion.
41. *The Interpretation of Dreams*, V:461.
42. *The Interpretation of Dreams*, V:460.
43. *The Interpretation of Dreams*, V:460.
44. *The Interpretation of Dreams*, V:460.

by beliefs and feelings. And it is the fact of having a strange emotional experience in our dreams—one that seems inappropriate to the content of the dream—which demands an intelligible account of our own emotions. Psychoanalytic interpretation removes the superficial appearance of irrationality in our emotional responses in dream life:

> In a dream I may be in a horrible, dangerous and disgusting situation without feeling any fear or repulsion; while another time, on the contrary, I may be terrified at something harmless and delighted at something childish. This particular enigma of dream-life vanishes more suddenly, perhaps, and more completely than any other, as soon as we pass over from the manifest to the latent content of the dream. We need not bother about the enigma, since it no longer exists. Analysis shows us that the ideational material has undergone displacements and substitutions, whereas the emotions have remained unaltered. It is small wonder that the ideational material, which has been changed by dream-distortion, should no longer be compatible with the emotion, which is retained unmodified; *nor is there anything left to be surprised at* after analysis has put the right material back into its former position.[45]

What analysis does, then, is to rescue the rationality of an emotion.

Freud recognized that this strategy is applicable to all cases of repression. Not only in dreams but in all neuroses, "the emotions are the constituent which is least influenced

---

45. *The Interpretation of Dreams*, V:460–61 (my emphasis). (Again, I use "emotion" rather than the Standard Edition's "affect.")

[by repression] and which alone can give us a pointer as to how we should fill in the missing thoughts."[46] For example, hysterics may be surprised to discover that they fear trivial things, mice or spiders, which they "know" they have no reason to fear.

> Psychoanalysis can put them upon the right path by recognizing the emotion as being, on the contrary, justified and by seeking out the idea which belongs to it but has been repressed and replaced by a substitute. A necessary premise to all this is that the release of emotion and the ideational content do not constitute the indissoluble organic unity as which we are in the habit of treating them, but that these two separate entities may be *merely soldered together* and can thus be detached from each other by analysis.[47]

The deeper point, which Freud ought to be making, is that an emotion and its appropriate idea *do* constitute an indissoluble organic unity. It is only on the surface of a dream that an emotion can be soldered onto almost any idea. Freud called this surface level, the dream-story that the analysand remembers, the "manifest content" of the dream. We are all familiar with the weirdest combinations of events and emotions in dreams. But when analysis penetrates deeper into the meaning of the dream—when it gets beyond the manifest level to what Freud called the *"latent content"* of the dream—it finds an underlying unity. It reveals that the emotion is *always* attached to its appropriate idea.

Repression, it seems, can never truly sunder an emotion from its idea. It may render the idea unconscious. But be-

46. *The Interpretation of Dreams*, V:461.
47. *The Interpretation of Dreams*, V:461–62 (my emphasis).

cause the idea remains alive and part of the emotion, a person may consciously experience certain fragments of the emotion. At the manifest level, an "inappropriate idea" may be "soldered" onto the emotion. But the inappropriate idea may be inappropriate *only from the perspective of the secondary-process mind* that is trying to understand. The emotion may be slipping along a path of loose associations. That is how it makes the journey from appropriate to inappropriate idea. Yet from the perspective of primary process, the journey has not led us astray. The "inappropriate idea" may, from the point of view of primary process, be just another expression of the very same thing as the "appropriate idea." The adult mind, functioning at the conceptual level of secondary process, may not recognize the similarity between the appropriate and inappropriate ideas. In that way, the emotional discharge with an inappropriate idea will escape repression. Archaic mind will thus achieve a disguised satisfaction. And it is because there is this similarity at the level of primary process that the inappropriate idea takes its place in consciousness. So, from the perspective of primary process, even the inappropriate idea has not been soldered onto the emotion. From this perspective, the inappropriate idea is just the appropriate idea which is indissolubly and organically linked with its emotion.

Once one sees this underlying unity, one is in a position to see that what is repressed is not merely an idea or a wish but an orientation to the world. The contents of the unconscious are emotions—at least, emotions conceived as orientations. This is how Freud actually treats the unconscious, though his theory cannot take it into account. For example, Freud says that the dream of the death of a loved one, accompanied by painful emotion, is due to an infantile wish that the loved one should die.[48] Thus the unconscious seems to be constituted by infantile wishes. However, when he describes the childhood scene in which that infantile wish was formed, it is clear that what the child is experiencing is not merely hostile desires but jealousy, love and envy. An emotion like jealousy is constituted by an evaluation that the person of whom one is jealous—a sibling, a parent— is a threat to the love that one would otherwise receive.[49] It is only against the background of this evaluation that the presence of a hostile wish is intelligible. And when Freud tries to persuade his reader that death dreams are due to unconscious death wishes, he does so by painting a picture of childhood in which such a death wish makes sense.[50] What Freud discovered, then, was not merely an unconscious infantile wish but an infantile orientation to the world.

The unconscious is of course not itself a unified orientation. The child may unconsciously love as well as hate the same person. The unconscious is, then, the home of disparate orientations to the world. One might even call them "proto-orientations." For we need the concept of an archaic ancestor of belief, just as wish is an ancestor of desire. The infantile "emotion" of jealousy requires both the proto-belief that a newborn has come to disrupt one's position in the family and a wish that the infant should disappear. But this proto-belief is not particularly responsive to further reality testing. It lives on long after one has come to a more mature orientation toward one's sibling. So if the infantile "emotion" is constituted by a proto-belief and a wish, rather

---

48. *The Interpretation of Dreams*, IV:248–67.
49. Cp. Aristotle's discussion of envy at *Rhetoric*, II.10.
50. See esp. *The Interpretation of Dreams*, IV:251, 258.

than by belief and desire, this "emotion," one might say, is not a full-fledged emotion, but a proto-emotion. The unconscious is the home of these infantile proto-emotions.

There are definite advantages to this conceptualization of the unconscious. It helps to explain the durability of infantile wishes: they are being sustained by rationalizing evaluations that are also cut off from reality-testing mechanisms and disconfirming beliefs. It also helps to explain how therapy might be therapeutic. For analysis allows these proto-beliefs and evaluations to develop into secondary-process formulations. They thus enter the arena of consciousness, where they can interact with other beliefs and evaluations. Insofar as they are diminished by these interactions, the wishes they have hitherto sustained are weakened. This conception of the unconscious also helps to explain the method of free association.[51] If the unconscious were a sea of isolated wishes, it would be a mystery why free association should lead back to them. Suppose, however, the wish is part of a structure of proto-beliefs, evaluations and wishes which has its own purposefulness, albeit hidden from conscious attention. These structures ramify out in all sorts of directions: a wish to get rid of a sibling is linked to a wish to recover parental love; and this in turn is due to a proto-belief about the relation between the sibling's appearance on the scene and loss of love, and so on. Thus once the conscious direction of attention is suspended, all roads should lead to the unconscious wish.

Freud, one might say, both underplayed and overplayed the rationality of the unconscious. On the one hand, the infantile wishes move along the loose paths of primary process, paying no heed to logical constraints. Thus viewed, it

---

51. Cp. *The Interpretation of Dreams*, V:529–31.

is a mystery how a secondary-process, conceptualizing mind could come to understand them. On the other hand, Freud thought that the infantile wish contained a hidden thought whose rationality primary process could not capture. Primary process does characterize what Freud called *the dream-work*: the process by which this latent dream-thought is distorted into the manifest dream. The dream-thought is hidden from view, because it is translated into a concrete image, condensed and displaced along a path of loose associations. The latent dream-thoughts, by contrast, "are immediately comprehensible, as soon as we have learnt them."[52]

> ... we are driven to conclude that two fundamentally different kinds of psychical process are concerned in the formation of dreams. One of these produces *perfectly rational dream-thoughts, of no less validity than normal thinking*: while the other treats these thoughts in a manner which is in the highest degree bewildering and irrational. We have already . . . segregated this second psychical process as being the dream-work proper.[53]

The task of interpretation, on this conception, is to work one's way back from the manifest dream, through the jumble of primary process, to a comprehensible set of wishes and beliefs.

---

52. *The Interpretation of Dreams*, IV:277.
53. *The Interpretation of Dreams*, V:597 (my emphasis). In the same passage he compares dreams to neurotic symptoms by saying that in both cases "rational thoughts have been subjected to irrational treatment." The underlying wish or belief is rational (though it may be poorly grounded); what is irrational is the chain of condensations, displacements, superficial associations that lead to the formation of a neurotic symptom.

We are here interested only in the essential dream-thoughts. These usually emerge as a complex of thoughts and memories of the most intricate possible structure, *with all the attributes of the trains of thought familiar to us in waking life.* . . . The restoration of the connections which the dream-work has destroyed is a task which has to be performed by the interpretative process.[54]

It was Freud's image of science that led him to this conclusion. He took himself to be discovering a reality that existed anyway, independently of the process of discovery. If what emerged from the analytic voyage was a thought with all the familiar attributes of waking life, it wasn't open to Freud to conclude that it was precisely because it *was* a thought of waking life—namely, Freud's own conscious interpretation—that it had those attributes. Psychoanalysis would not be a science if it were not discovering these already existing thoughts in the unconscious. Thus he overrationalized the unconscious dream-thought. And he underrationalized primary process. Since Freud thought there already was a fully rational thought in the unconscious, he could split off primary process and treat it as the incarnation of irrationality.

Thus instead of viewing archaic mental activity as the

---

54. *The Interpretation of Dreams*, IV: 311–12. Cp. V:506: "The dream-thoughts are entirely rational . . ." See also "Fragment of an Analysis of a Case of Hysteria": "In my *Interpretation of Dreams* . . . I showed that dreams in general can be interpreted and that after the work of interpretation has been completed they can be replaced by perfectly correctly constructed thoughts which can be assigned a recognizable position in the chain of mental events. . . . [In treating neurotics] I learnt how to translate the language of dreams into the forms of expression of our own thought-language which can be understood without further help" (VII:12). And see "A Note on the Unconscious in Psycho-Analysis" (XII:265): "The latent thoughts of the dream differ in no respect from the products of our regular conscious activity."

subject of a science of subjectivity, Freud's conception of science led him to conceive archaic mind as a distorting force. For the author of *The Interpretation of Dreams*, archaic mental activity is dream-*work*; a force which hides and clouds the true subject of the science: a fully rational, but unconscious thought. In order to have conceived of archaic mind as what his science is about, Freud would have had to reconceive what a science is. Archaic expressions of mind are by their nature unfinished, and the understanding of those expressions seems to complete a process which germinated in archaic expressions, to be sure, but which does not flower until those expressions have been taken up and understood. If science is to treat archaic mind as its subject matter, the science should be conceived as growing out of and completing the archaic expressions it is striving to understand. Here is one way to link the idea of a science of subjectivity with the idea that archaic mind is what this science is about: posit a basic developmental force in nature of which archaic mind and the science that understands that mind are both manifestations. The transition from archaic mental activity to a mature understanding of that activity may then itself be viewed as a manifestation of this developmental force. It was not until twenty years after he published *The Interpretation of Dreams* that Freud's own unfolding conceptual development would lead him to posit such a force. In so doing he would break with the model of science to which he was devoted; but before doing so, Freud's therapeutic practice and his theoretical self-understanding would have to stand apart.

4

Interpretation and Transformation: The Case of Little Hans

I

If there is a puzzle about the nature of an infantile wish, it is worth turning to Freud's study of little Hans; for if there is a gap between Freud's practice and theory, it is in the details of a case history that we might be able to discover it. And it is in this study that Freud tries to capture the infantile wish as it exists in the infant's soul.

Surely there must be a possibility of observing in children at first hand and in all the freshness of life the sexual impulses and wishes which we dig out so laboriously in adults from among their own debris—especially as it is also our belief that they are the common property of all men, a part of the human constitution, and merely exaggerated or distorted in the case of neurotics.[1]

1. "Analysis of a Phobia in A Five Year Old Boy," X:6.

But it is not at all clear how to understand the sexual impulses and wishes which we "observe" in children. Consider, for example, Hans's interest in his "widdler."[2] According to the case history, Hans's earliest investigations into nature focused on the possession of widdlers. Hans asked his mother and father if they too had a widdler, to which they each responded affirmatively; he said of a cow being milked that the milk was coming out of its widdler; in response to a threat that he would have his widdler cut off if he kept touching it, he said that he would in that case widdle with his bottom; he remarked, upon seeing chamber pots of blood in his parents' bedroom after the birth of his sister, "but blood doesn't come out of my widdler"; he remarked upon seeing his seven-day-old sister being given a bath that her widdler was quite small.[3] In his discussion of this case, Freud says:

> The first trait in little Hans which can be regarded as part of his sexual life was a quite peculiarly lively interest in his "widdler"—an organ deriving its name from that one of its two functions which, scarcely the less important of the two, is not to be eluded in the nursery. This interest aroused in him the spirit of enquiry, and he thus discovered that the presence or absence of a widdler made it possible to differentiate between animate and inanimate objects. He assumed that all animate objects were like himself, and possessed this important bodily organ; he observed that it was present in the larger animals, suspected that this was so too in both his parents, and was not deterred

2. "Analysis of a Phobia in A Five Year Old Boy," X:7.
3. "Analysis of a Phobia in A Five Year Old Boy," X:7–11.

by the evidence of his own eyes from authenticating the fact in his new-born sister. One might almost say that it would have been too shattering a blow to his "*Weltanschauung*" if he had had to make up his mind to forego the presence of this organ in a being similar to him; it would have been as though it were being torn away from himself.[4]

According to Freud, little Hans, like many a scientist, is willing to misinterpret the observational evidence rather than abandon his theory.[5] But how does Freud know that this is what Hans is doing? He assumes that by "widdler" Hans means penis, but what grounds this assumption? There does seem to be some evidence in favor. Hans refers to his own penis as a widdler, as he does to the penises of animals he sees in the zoo; he speculates that his mother has a big widdler like a horse; and when he draws a widdler on a giraffe, it is a straight line down from the giraffe's underside.[6] Penises, it is plausible to say, are widdlers. However, Hans also refers to a cow's udder as a widdler, he observes that his newborn sister has a very small widdler and says, apparently nonchalantly, that if his widdler were cut off, he would widdle with his bottom. In virtue of what are we to say that Hans has made a mistake about the cow? Or his sister? Why aren't udders and vaginas and, indeed, bottoms that widdle also widdlers?

For Hans to have made a mistake about cows, it seems he must have a determinate concept of a widdler, in which a widdler is a penis. His mistake is then one of observation:

---

4. "Analysis of a Phobia in A Five Year Old Boy," X:106.
5. Cp. Quine, "Two Dogmas of Empiricism," in *From a Logical Point of View*; Kuhn, *The Structure of Scientific Revolutions*.
6. "Analysis of a Phobia in A Five Year Old Boy," X:10–13.

he takes the milking of a cow to be through a penis. But in virtue of what can we attribute to Hans such a determinate concept? Whether we look inside or outside the mind, it is not obvious how we can answer this question. Suppose we begin on the inside and look for an idea of a widdler in Hans's mind.[7] Of course, it is not clear what we mean by an "idea." If by "idea" we just mean "belief," then we are back with our original question, trying to determine what Hans believes about widdlers. Suppose, then, that Hans's "idea" of a widdler is a mental image of a penis. There is nothing about this image that would direct Hans to apply the term "widdler" only to penises. Even if Hans is supposed to apply "widdler" only to things that look like his mental image, what it is for something to *look like* his image depends on his sense of similarity. There is no absolute standard of similarity independent of people's judgments of similarity. Therefore, if a cow's udder looks to Hans like his image of a widdler, there is no basis for saying that Hans had made a mistake. The mental image alone gives no ground for saying that, for Hans, "widdler" means penis.[8]

In fact, Freud began by looking outside the mind. For to say that Hans has made a mistake about widdlers is

7. The theory that ideas in the mind give verbal expressions meaning has a classic expression in Locke's *An Essay Concerning Human Understanding*, Book III. The classic undermining of this theory is to be found in Wittgenstein's *Philosophical Investigations*, to which this discussion is heavily indebted. For a study of the relation of Locke's theory of meaning to the later Wittgenstein, see Hacker, *Insight and Illusion: Wittgenstein on Philosophy and the Metaphysics of Experience*.

8. Alternatively, one might suppose that Hans's idea is the embedded rules which direct his use of the expression "widdler." Unlike a mental image, this type of idea is not something that by its nature is at least potentially available to consciousness. And so the only route to these rules is by inference from Hans's linguistic behavior. Therefore, there can be no basis for citing his linguistic behavior as making a mistake about his idea; for it is only from the behavior that we can determine what the idea is.

implicitly to assume that Hans is willing to correct his understanding to conform to the community's understanding of what a penis is. Hans, one might say, wants to mean penis by "widdler," but he doesn't yet understand what a penis is. His "mistake," then, is not that his use of "widdler" conflicts with the idea in *his* mind. It is, rather, that both his idea and his linguistic behavior are out of step with the community that he is in the process of joining. His "mistake" consists in being a child. There may be value in taking "widdler" to mean penis if one's aim is to bring the child into a natural language community. For one will eventually correct the child's use of "widdler" when it deviates from ordinary use of "penis": and one will thus educate the child into the language. But this strategy defeats our purpose. We don't want to educate Hans; we want to understand the contents of an infantile mind.

One way to get to these contents might be to treat Hans as forming a community of one. The meaning of "widdler" would then be given by what Hans does and would call a "widdler."[9] The focus on Hans's actual and potential use will give us Hans's disposition to call things "widdlers." But there is a problem which confronts any attempt to determine what this disposition is. Would Hans call an elephant's trunk a widdler? An anteater's nose? A large draining cyst? An octopus's tendril? We have no way of answering these questions. *We* may see a certain coherence in Hans's way of going on, but it is not sufficient for us to feel confident that we can go on to use the expression in respect to these problematic cases. More importantly, there does not seem to be any way to investigate what the disposition is without possibly altering it. Suppose, for in-

---

9. Cp. Wittgenstein, *Philosophical Investigations*, I.187.

stance, that Hans had called an elephant's trunk a widdler. Is there any room for thinking that he might have made a mistake, even by his own lights? Suppose that we pointed out to Hans that this elephant also had a penis or a vagina; suppose, too, that we showed Hans that the elephant urinated through his penis, and that he used his trunk both as an olfactory and as a prehensile organ. It is not clear how Hans would respond. He might decide that the elephant has two widdlers. But let us suppose that he revises his original judgment: he comes to deny that the trunk is a widdler and asserts that the penis is one. There is no way to decide whether Hans has corrected a mistake in his own use of "widdler" or whether he has revised the concept of a widdler in the light of our teaching.

There is, then, a severe limit to the extent to which anyone can go native in a tribe that consists of one three-and-a-half-year-old speaker. Any attempt to focus in on what he means will to some extent draw his attention to our perceptions of salience. In trying to enter his linguistic community, we inevitably draw him into ours. There seems to be a gap that cannot be completely closed between the conceptual content of a mental state and the content of an infant's mind.

II

The point of these reflections is not to insist upon the ineffability of the infantile mind, but to help us understand what is involved in making a psychoanalytic interpretation of a symptom, fantasy or dream in terms of infantile wishes. To that end, we must look to the material out of which Freud fashioned his interpretations. It seems that Freud had two related phenomena to work with: the transformation of little Hans's emotions and the development of his fantasies. Hans came to Freud's attention due to his transformation from being happy and inquisitive into being a shy, then anxious, then phobic little boy. Freud attributed the outbreak of anxiety to the increase and subsequent repression of Hans's affection for his mother.[10] This repression transformed his longing into a voracious anxiety capable of swallowing up Hans's emotional life.[11] For poor Hans, there had been a "general reversal of pleasure into unpleasure which had come over the whole of his sexual researches."[12] Freud attributed this reversal to Hans's realization that his own widdler was distressingly small in comparison to an adult widdler. "But," Freud adds, "*since the whole train of thought was probably incapable of becoming clearly conscious*, this distressing feeling, too, was transformed into anxiety, so that his present anxiety was erected both upon his former pleasure and his present unpleasure."[13]

Why was this train of thought incapable of becoming clearly conscious? One answer is that the thought is repressed. It cannot thus rise up into Hans's consciousness. Another answer is that repression prevents the thought from forming. On the first account, Hans has a certain thought which he cannot think; on the second account, Hans does not and cannot have that thought, and that is why he cannot think it. Freud lends some support to both accounts. Insofar as he conceives himself as a scientific investigator of a hitherto undiscovered reality which exists independently of the investigation, Freud tends to treat the unconscious thought

10. "Analysis of a Phobia in A Five Year Old Boy," X:25.
11. "Analysis of a Phobia in A Five Year Old Boy," X:26, 32.
12. "Analysis of a Phobia in A Five Year Old Boy," X:34.
13. "Analysis of a Phobia in A Five Year Old Boy," X:34–35 (my emphasis).

as fully formed and hidden. But he sometimes suggests that the way repression is able to keep a thought unconscious is by preventing it from developing into a fully fledged thought. The unconscious, Freud realized, operates at a different representational level from consciousness. The concrete, imagistic unconscious represents the thing. For a thought to become conscious, this thing-representation must be linked with an appropriate word-representation. Freud called this process of linking "transference."[14] Basically, the energy attaching to the unconscious idea—an archaic thing-representation—is transferred onto the secondary-process concept. The conscious or preconscious thought thus acquires "an undeserved degree of intensity."[15] Of course, Freud used the term "transference" in myriad ways, often to pick out one of a family of related processes. Let us call this particular process, by which an unconscious archaic representation is linked with a secondary-process concept, *intrapsychic transference*, or transference *within the mind*. For an unconscious thought to become conscious, Freud believed, it must develop into "a higher psychical organization."[16]

If Freud had spent more time thinking about this process of development, it might have led him to refine his conception of intrapsychic transference. For, as Freud himself pointed out, archaic mind is distinguished both by its

14. *The Interpretation of Dreams*, V:562–64.
15. *The Interpretation of Dreams*, V:563. Thus Freud came to call this process "hypercathexis" or "hyperinvestment": see "The Unconscious," XIV:201–2. This is discussed by Loewald in *Papers on Psychoanalysis*, pp. 181–95, 245–54.
16. "The Unconscious," XIV:202. One might wonder: if Freud recognized that the unconscious functions with archaic representations, how could he also have thought that the latent contents of dreams were "perfectly rational dream-thoughts, of no less validity than normal thinking"? The answer is that it took time even to begin to work through the radical consequences of his discovery of archaic mental functioning.

"thing-representations"—its concrete, imagistic form—and by its loose associations. Primitive mental activity slips along a path of "thing-representations" which, from the point of view of secondary-process thinking, have only the most superficial similarities. Archaic associations typically look bizarre to the secondary-process mind that is trying to understand them. But if that is so, the "higher psychical organization" required for consciousness cannot consist solely in the attachment of a word to a thing-representation. The thing-representations themselves must be disciplined so that a word can legitimately be applied. That is, a distinction must be made among the associated thing-representations between those that are instances of the concept expressed by the word and those that are (from the point of view of secondary process) only loosely associated to it. This is a distinction that can only be made at the level of secondary process. From the perspective of archaic mind, the loose associations don't appear loose, they just appear associated. Thus the transition of a "thought" from the unconscious to the conscious would not just consist in the attachment of a word to a thing-representation; it would consist in the acquisition of a concept. And this acquisition would partially consist in segregating those thing-representations that genuinely fall under the concept. The unconscious thought, then, is not merely concrete and imagistic; it is only on its way toward being a candidate for a concept. It is not yet a developed thought, though it is something that could develop into a developed thought.

Intrapsychic transference, therefore, should be conceived not as the mere attachment of a word to a thing-representation, but as the incorporation of a concept at the level of both word and thing. The word expresses the concept, the things have been differentiated so as to instantiate the concept, and the concept and things have been linked together. This is the development of a higher psychical organization: an organization that is occurring equally at archaic and higher levels of mental activity.

Consider, for example, the emergence of Hans's fear of horses. The outbreak of the phobia was preceded by a period of anxiety, which, as we have seen, Freud attributed to Hans's repressed longing for his mother.[17] There is a sense in which anxiety lacks conceptualization: it is fear of an unconceptualized object. And, Freud argues, anxiety naturally strives toward conceptualization: by its nature it tends to look for an object and thus transform itself into fear.[18] Although Freud says an emotion is a discharge of psychical energy, he treats it as an orientation to the world. The difference between anxiety and fear is characterized by Freud in terms of Hans's relation to the world. His anxiety was free-floating; his fear was of horses. And the transformation of emotion required no more than settling on an object to be fearful of. Freud offered a psychological explanation of this transformation.[19] Because of its lack of direction there is no obvious defense against anxiety; but once anxiety has found an object and thus transformed itself into fear, it is possible for the person to take protective measures to avoid the fearful object.

But how did Hans settle on horses? It occurred, Freud said, by a process of "transference."[20] In this case, transference is not an intrapsychic relation; it involves a person's

---

17. The early Freud would attribute this anxiety to the breaking through of repressed sexual energy; the later Freud would attribute it to the ego setting off a danger signal. See *Inhibitions, Symptoms and Anxiety*, XX:87–174.

18. "Analysis of a Phobia in A Five Year Old Boy," X:26, 116–17.

19. "Analysis of a Phobia in A Five Year Old Boy," X:116–17.

20. "Analysis of a Phobia in A Five Year Old Boy," X:51. Cp. *The Interpretation of Dreams*, V:562.

orientation to the world. Basically, a meaningful emotional response can be transferred onto seemingly inappropriate objects through a series of loose associations that characterize archaic mental activity. Hans lived in an environment that was, as it were, peopled with horses.[21] He lived across the street from a warehouse to which horse-drawn carts drew up all day long. Given this environmental accident, horses did offer a suitable symbolic vehicle through which to channel his emotional life. Horses are big, and they have big widdlers. They also have big "lumfs": excrement, which Hans speculated may be the way babies are produced.[22] Thus they were not only early objects of fascination in his exploration of the world of widdlers; they suitably represent a big father in comparison with little Hans. Hans's first "horse" had been his father. Horses also bite. They can thus take revenge on a little boy for his oedipal wishes. But the terrifying event that triggered the phobia occurred when Hans went out for a walk with his mother one day and saw a big horse, drawing a bus, fall down. He no doubt associated to his father having fallen down, and perhaps feared the strength of his own oedipal wishes.[23]

On Freud's scientific image, a fear of the father has been

21. Here I give only the briefest outline of the horse-associations (mainly from X:48–52, 125–27). There is no substitute for reading the case history to get the flavor of the associations.

22. "Analysis of a Phobia in A Five Year Old Boy," X:63–75.

23. This traumatic event also reinforced and reenacted a deeper association between horses and falling down. In an early childhood game of horses, his playmate Fritz, "of whom he was so fond, but at the same time, perhaps his rival with many girl friends," had hit his foot against a stone and fallen down (X:126; cp. 58–59). Falling down also served to link the family of associations around horses to a family of associations to do with what Hans called "lumfs." Lumfs are the sort of things that fall down; indeed, his sister Hanna was a lumf who had been born, not stork-brought, from his heavily laden mother. Indeed, horse-drawn carts were lumf-loaded, and thus the horse falling down could at once represent the death of his father, the birth of his sister and the death of his mother in childbirth.

transferred onto horses. Repression consists in sundering the idea of the father and attaching the emotion to another object. On the developmental model, by contrast, that which would have resolved itself into fear of the father is prevented from doing so. Repression consists in inhibiting this process of resolution and in promoting the wrong sort of conceptualization. But it is not that the conscious idea of a horse is substituted for the unconscious idea of the father. Rather, for Hans's unconscious, there is no significant difference between fathers and horses. Father-representations and horse-representations are, one might say, "lumfed" together. Because of repression, the horse-representations are differentiated out of a plethora of loose associations.

On this view, intrapsychic transference is always the drawing in of boundaries around a family of resemblances that cannot be fully contained within a concept. Philosophers tend to think that what hold us together as a linguistic community are our shared perceptions of similarity and relevance, our shared routes of interest and feelings of naturalness.[24] Freud shows that there is a realm of shared perceptions of similarity that tend to be overlooked by conscious thought. The meaning of "horse" is not exhausted by all the things we are disposed to call horses. If we "look and see" all the things we call horses, we will only discover the manifest content of the concept.[25] We will miss the family resemblances to all those things we are not disposed to call "horses" but which invest horses with significance for us. It is remarkable how Hans's train of associations through fathers to horses and lumfs appears at once so bi-

---

24. This is one lesson of Wittgenstein's *Philosophical Investigations*; it has been well described by Stanley Cavell in "The Availability of Wittgenstein's Later Philosophy," in *Must We Mean What We Say?* I discuss this further in Chapter 6.

25. Cp. *Philosophical Investigations*, I.66.

zarre and so natural to us. Freud doesn't even have to argue
for the associations; he need only present it for it to take on
a certain plausibility. In this world of archaic associations
horses are fathers and mothers and lumf carriers. It is these
hidden but natural-seeming family resemblances that give
secondary-process concepts their archaic, imaginative
content.

Freud's therapy consisted in promoting a different intrapsychic transference. He waited until Hans produced a
fantasy that allowed an alternative conceptualization. This
opportunity came with Hans's fantasy of two giraffes: " '*In
the night there was a big giraffe in the room and a crumpled
one; and the big one called out because I took the crumpled
one away from it. Then it stopped calling out; and then I sat
down on top of the crumpled one.*' "[26] This was the clearest
expression of Hans's oedipal wishes to date, and Freud decided it was time to interpret Hans's fear of horses: "the
horse," he told Hans, "must be his father whom he had good
internal reasons for fearing."[27]

I . . . disclosed to him that he was afraid of his father,
precisely because he was so fond of his mother. It must
be, I told him, that he thought his father was angry
with him on that account; but this was not so, his
father was fond of him in spite of it, and he might
admit everything to him without any fear. Long before
he was in the world, I went on, I had known that a
little Hans would come who would be so fond of his
mother that he would be bound to feel afraid of his
father because of it; and I had told his father this.[28]

26. "Analysis of a Phobia in A Five Year Old Boy," X:37.
27. "Analysis of a Phobia in A Five Year Old Boy," X:123.
28. "Analysis of a Phobia in A Five Year Old Boy," X:42.

Freud's interpretation offered Hans a set of concepts with which he could understand his own productions. The giraffe fantasy was critical for Freud, for it virtually presents itself in conceptual form. Thus, in addition to concepts, Freud is able to offer Hans an opportunity for linking these concepts to the archaic productions which the concepts rationalize.

Freud also offered Hans reassurance. What was happening to him was natural, it could be understood with care and concern. Most importantly, he need fear neither his father's revenge nor the loss of his love. His father understood him and loved him. From the beginning of his supervision of the case, Freud sought to bring about an emotional transformation. Hans is repeatedly assured by his parents that there is a doctor who understands what is happening and who can help him. An atmosphere is established in the home that is concerned and caring, reassuring and understanding. It is in this environment that Hans's fantasy life can develop in articulation until he has the fantasy of two giraffes. It would seem that the environment allowed mental development to resume. When the formulations of archaic mind get close to a secondary-process expression, Freud gives his interpretation. The interpretation offers Hans an alternative set of concepts with which to understand his infantile wishes, it offers an opportunity of linking concepts to the archaic wishes, and it offers Hans the opportunity to transform his emotional relationship to those wishes. Freud reports that his interpretation was remarkably efficacious: "a possibility had now been offered him of bringing forward his unconscious productions and of unfolding his phobia."[29]

---

29. "Analysis of a Phobia in A Five Year Old Boy," X:43; see also X:123.

Intrapsychic transference is the fulfillment of this possibility. And if we think of an emotion as containing its own conceptualization, then this intrapsychic transference is in effect the development of Hans's emotional life. He is not just finding the proper concepts to apply to the emotional "objects" in his life; the emotional "objects" are acquiring their own conceptualization. For this to be possible, Hans must transform the emotional relation in which he stands to his own wishes. He no longer fears his oedipal wishes; he can acknowledge and accept them. This allows the wishes themselves to develop in form and content: that is, to move in the direction of becoming desires. This in turn allows the proto-emotions of the unconscious to develop into emotions. The transformation of Hans's emotional life and the transformation of Hans's understanding of his emotional life are of a piece. This would suggest that the development of mental functioning from archaic to a genuine secondary-process understanding of the archaic requires a certain emotional well-being. The development of mental functioning is an expression of that well-being. In fact, much of what Freud says about the content of Hans's wishes is compatible with this conception. For example, Freud says:

> Therapeutic success . . . is not our primary aim; we endeavour rather to enable the patient to obtain a conscious grasp of his unconscious wishes. And this we can achieve by working upon the basis of hints he throws out, and so, with the help of our interpretative technique, presenting the unconscious complex to his consciousness *in our own words*. There will be *a certain degree of similarity* between that which he hears from us and that which he is looking for, and which, in spite of all the resistances, is trying to force its way through

to consciousness; and *it is this similarity* that will enable him to discover the unconscious material.[30]

By presenting his unconscious complex to his consciousness "in our own words," Freud is, on this developmental interpretation, giving Hans a set of concepts with which to think about his wishes. This does more than enable Hans to conceive of a reality that existed *in toto* antecedently to his newfound ability: it enables him to conceptualize his wishes in a certain way. The wishes themselves absorb this conceptualization and thus enter into commerce with secondary-process thinking. That is, the wishes develop into desires: or, at least, the wishes enter into commerce with desires. Of course, there must be a certain similarity—a family resemblance—between the primary-process fantasy and the secondary-process concept which interprets it: only thus can the fantasy be understood; only thus can the interpretation be therapeutic. Family resemblances thus run not merely across primary-process associations or through the instances of a secondary-process concept; they run between primary-process associations and the secondary-process concepts which interpret them.

Freud's role, on this developmental interpretation, is to complete a process of development: to supply the concepts toward which a process of mental and emotional growth is striving and thereby to give the meaning of that very process. At times, Freud seems to suggest such a role for himself:

It is true that during the analysis Hans had to be told many things that he could not say himself, that he had

---

30. "Analysis of a Phobia in A Five Year Old Boy," X:120–21 (Freud's emphasis and mine).

to be presented with thoughts which he had so far shown no signs of possessing, and that his attention had to be turned in the direction from which his father was expecting something to come. This detracts from the evidential value of the analysis; but the procedure is the same in every case. For a psycho-analysis is not an impartial scientific investigation, but a therapeutic measure. Its essence is not to prove anything, but merely to alter something. In a psycho-analysis the physician always gives his patient (sometimes to a greater and sometimes to a lesser extent) the conscious anticipatory ideas by the help of which he is put in a position to recognize and to grasp the unconscious material. For there are some patients who need more of such assistance and some who need less; but there are none who get through without some of it.[31]

It is of course possible to understand this role in terms of the classical conception of psychoanalytic theory: an analytic interpretation uncovers an unconscious wish. But it is preferable to understand it in terms of the developmental model: an analytic interpretation helps to direct and complete a process of mental development. Many of Freud's remarks about analytic interpretation are open to such a dual understanding. For example, Freud says that he had to interpret a series of Hans's fantasies in terms of the same oedipal wishes:

> We must not be surprised to find *the same wishes* constantly reappearing in the course of an analysis. The monotony only attaches to the analyst's interpretations

31. "Analysis of a Phobia in A Five Year Old Boy," X:104. Incidentally, I think this is a franker account of the role of therapy in psychoanalysis than that given in the previous quotation.

of these wishes. *For Hans they were not mere repetitions, but steps in a progressive development* from timid hinting to fully conscious, undistorted perspicuity.[32]

The "progressive development" may be understood in classical terms as the progressive revelation to consciousness of the already existing oedipal wishes, but it may also be understood as the progressive development in the content of the wishes themselves. One reason that the classical understanding is tempting is that there seems to be *some one thing* that underlies, causes and explains the disparate phenomena. Hans's repressed oedipal wishes, one wants to say, are responsible for *all* the myriad fantasies and transformations of emotion reported in the case history. Indeed, it is in virtue of this underlying thing that psychoanalysis is explanatory and potentially therapeutic. What better underlying thing could there be than a wish that is generating fantasy after fantasy, symptom after symptom?

It is crucial to realize that one does not have to adhere to the classical understanding of psychoanalysis in order to accept this plausible line of reasoning. Even if there is an underlying thing—an unconscious wish—that is generating a succession of fantasies and symptoms, it does not follow that the wish must exist from the beginning in completed form. The wish, too, may be undergoing a development, a development which is manifested in the succession of fantasies it causes and completed by the internalization of a secondary-process analytic interpretation. Freud says that "while the analysis of a case is in progress it is impossible to obtain any clear impression of the structure and development of the neurosis."[33] On the classical understanding,

---

32. "Analysis of a Phobia in A Five Year Old Boy," X:130 (my emphasis).
33. "Analysis of a Phobia in A Five Year Old Boy," X:132.

this is attributed to the fact that analysis has not uncovered the underlying structure; the current suggestion is that it is not until the end of an analysis that the underlying structure is fully developed.

But if an infantile wish may develop in content over time, how are we to see its various manifestations as all productions of the same wish? Freud's implicit procedure is developmental. He expects the symptoms to develop in complexity and articulation, from vaguely formed anxiety, to fear of horses, to a worked-out oedipal fantasy of two giraffes. Freud relies on our ability, as interpreters, to recognize a family resemblance among the disparate archaic productions. We can see similarities that link the anxiety to the fear of horses to the fantasy of the crumpled giraffe to the falling lumf . . . The analyst's interpretation provides the concepts with which the unity of these myriad primary-process productions can be understood. This intrapsychic transference does not subsume all of the primary-process material under concepts. Fear of horses, for example, is not, strictly speaking, fear of the father. And yet, the fear of horses is not just left behind. A link is established between the secondary-process concept "fear of father" and the primary-process fear of horses that does not, strictly speaking, fall under it. That is what makes the interpretation an intrapsychic transference, and it is in terms of this relation that the primary-process material can be understood. Because the analytic interpretation seems so genuinely unifying of disparate phenomena, it is tempting to think that the infantile wish *in the form stated by the analyst* must have been there all along directing the production of the phenomena. But this temptation ought to be resisted. There is no reason to think that this wish must exist from the beginning in its final, conceptualized form.[34]

Freud's intervention, as we have seen, had a dramatic effect on the unfolding of Hans's fantasy and emotional life.[35] Although Freud gives his interpretation in secondary-process, conceptual terms, Hans manifests both his neurosis *and his cure* in emotional transformations and archaic fantasies. In his final triumphal fantasies, Hans has not only been equipped with a bigger widdler and succeeded in marrying his mother, he has overcome the threat of a vengeful father by marrying him off to *his* mother.[36] "With this fantasy," Freud says, "both the illness and the analysis came to an appropriate end."[37] On the classical conception, the success of the analysis is due to the undoing of the repression of the infantile wish.[38] But there is also a transformation in the content of the wish: the father-horse is no longer feared in part because his fantasied role has been transformed into one in which he no longer has any reason to seek revenge. The analytic interpretation, therefore, not only provides concepts for the archaic productions; it helps to shape the course of those productions.

Conversely, the loose associations of archaic mind help to provide the content of the analytic interpretation. In-

34. This is a mistake which itself bears a family resemblance to a mistake that Wittgenstein warned us against: namely, of thinking that because we can recognize certain similarities among all the disparate things we call "games" there must be an underlying essence which all these games have in common. Note that Wittgenstein does not deny that there is an underlying *something* which links all the disparate things we are willing to call "games." But this something is not, for Wittgenstein, an underlying essence which renders intelligible what it is to be a game; it is, rather, our underlying and innate sense of similarity and relevance: our ability to see certain resemblances among these disparate activities. See *Philosophical Investigations*, e.g., I.67–71.
35. See, e.g., "Analysis of a Phobia in A Five Year Old Boy," X:43, 123.
36. "Analysis of a Phobia in A Five Year Old Boy," X:96–98, 131–32.
37. "Analysis of a Phobia in A Five Year Old Boy," X:132.
38. See, e.g., "Analysis of a Phobia in A Five Year Old Boy," X:145.

trapsychic transference works from the bottom up as well as from the top down. It is only if we look to the succession of fantasies and symptoms, the transformations of the emotions, that we can understand what is meant by oedipal love and hate. This may help to explain why, to put it in Freud's terms, knowledge is not sufficient for cure.[39] Freud discovered early in his career that merely informing a patient of his unconscious conflicts often leads to an exacerbation of the neurotic symptoms. One must prepare the ground for an analytic interpretation. Otherwise it will increase the patient's resistances rather than help in overcoming them. For the interpretation to be therapeutic, Freud said, "the patient must, through preparation, himself have reached the neighborhood of what he has repressed."[40] It is by now widely accepted analytic technique that an interpretation can only be a step ahead of the patient if it is to be therapeutic. The developmental account of intrapsychic transference helps to explain why this should be so. If the loose associations of archaic mind help to invest the interpretation with the meaning it has, then if one is not yet in a position to see these productions as instances of, say, oedipal love and hate, one is not yet in a position to understand the meaning of the interpretation. On this developmental account, *knowledge is sufficient for cure.* The problem with a prematurely uttered, but accurate interpretation is that the person who hears it is not in a position to understand what is being said.[41] The question now arises as to what is involved in seeing the archaic production as an instance of an oedipal emotion. The developmental account thus provides a shift of focus. Instead of asking "what in addition to knowl-

---

39. See, e.g., " 'Wild' Psycho-Analysis," XI:225.
40. " 'Wild' Psycho-Analysis," XI:225.
41. I discuss this further in Chapter 6.

edge is required?" we now ask "what is required in order to have knowledge?"[42] A necessary condition for knowledge is understanding, and understanding is a richer and deeper notion than we might initially have expected.

The meaning of an infantile wish, therefore, is grounded both in the loose associations of archaic mind and in the analytic interpretation that completes the development of the wish as it renders it intelligible. And this, in turn, solves the puzzle of the intelligibility of infantile wishes. We render this mental force intelligible by imposing an adult, analytic, secondary-process judgment on it. Yet though an imposition, it is not an arbitrary imposition: indeed, it is the archaic manifestations of the infantile wish that give content to the interpretation.

---

42. Cp. Freud: "I dislike making use of analytic writings as an assistance to my patients; I require them to learn by personal experience, and I assure them that they will acquire wider and more valuable knowledge than the whole literature of psychoanalysis could teach them." "Recommendations to Physicians Practicing Psychoanalysis," XII: 119–20.

5

What Is Sex?

I

It was in the smells and feels, the secretions, inhibitions and fantasies of sexual life that Freud discovered a developmental force in human nature. That is, Freud happened upon sexuality in its more archaic manifestations. At first he took sexuality to be unproblematic: what was surprising was the extent to which sexuality spread throughout psychological life. Eventually, however, Freud had to call sexuality into question: what is this force that exerts such a powerful influence in human life? Sexuality itself stands in need of an interpretation. Just as an interpretation of a person's infantile wishes helps to complete a process of development, so an interpretation of sexuality helps to complete a development within psychoanalysis. That development began with the recognition of sexuality's archaic expressions, and it is completed by an understanding of their significance. And just as a person's wishes are not abolished, but infuse an interpretation with meaning, so the primitive expressions of sexuality give life to the concept of sexuality.

Freud began with the idea that sexuality is a drive. The problem is that he did not know what a drive is or what it is for a drive to be sexual. Throughout his career, he expresses doubt that he has understood what a drive is; and his introduction of the concept of a drive reflects his uncertainty.[1]

> By a "drive" is provisionally to be understood *the psychical representative* of an endosomatic, continuously flowing source of stimulation, as contrasted with a "stimulus," which is set up by single excitations coming from without. The concept of drive is thus one of those lying on the frontier between the mental and the physical. The simplest and likeliest assumption as to the nature of drives would seem to be that *in itself a drive is without quality*, and, so far as mental life is concerned, is only to be regarded as a measure of the demand made upon the mind for work.[2]

1. See, e.g., the footnote added to *Three Essays on the Theory of Sexuality* in 1924: "The theory of the drives is the most important but at the same time the least complete portion of psychoanalytic theory" (VII:168 n.). Remarks like this pepper Freud's work. Cp., e.g., "On Narcissism: An Introduction" (1914): "In the total absence of any theory of the drives which would help us to find our bearings, we may be permitted, or rather, it is incumbent upon us, to start off by working out some hypothesis to its logical conclusion, until it either breaks down or is confirmed" (XIV:78); "Instincts and Their Vicissitudes" (1915): "I am altogether doubtful whether any decisive pointers for the differentiation and classification of the drives can be arrived at on the basis of working over the psychological material" (XIV:124); *Beyond the Pleasure Principle* (1920): "The most abundant sources of this internal excitation are what are described as the organism's 'drives' . . . at once the most important and the most obscure element of psychological research" (XVIII:34); "In the obscurity that reigns at present in the theory of drives, it would be unwise to reject any idea that promises to throw light on it" (XVIII:53); *Inhibitions, Symptoms and Anxiety* (1926): "It is almost humiliating that, after working so long, we should still be having difficulty in understanding the most fundamental facts. . . . What is hampering us here is evidently some hitch in the development of our theory of the drives" (XX:124). (See also "Psycho-Analytic Notes on an Autobiographical Account of a Case of Paranoia," XII:74.)

2. *Three Essays on the Theory of Sexuality*, VII:168 (my emphasis).

Humans, Freud discovered, are pressured to live. The drives are continuous, internal sources of pressure. Yet Freud is clearly having trouble capturing the frontier quality of the drives. For, on the one hand, he introduces the drive as the *psychical representative* of a physiological force. But, on the other hand, he says that "in itself the drive is without quality": and this suggests that he is identifying the drive with the physiological force itself. It looks as though Freud is at one moment placing the drive on one side of the frontier, and the next moment placing it on the other.[3] This doesn't do justice to the possibility that a drive may straddle the border. It may even call into question the idea of a sharp boundary.

It is, of course, unsatisfying simply to convict Freud of an inconsistency. He is clearly struggling to formulate a concept that does justice both to the psychological and to the purely physiological properties of drives. But if a drive has psychological as well as physiological aspects, we can try to consider the psychological aspects of the drive in isolation. The drive *considered psychologically* is a mental stimulus, an item in the mind, a psychical representative of biological stimuli. The drive *considered physiologically* is a purely physiological process.[4] Here we may not be dealing

---

3. This uncertainty remains fairly constant in Freud's work. Ten years later, in "Instincts and Their Vicissitudes," he says: "If now we apply ourselves to considering mental life from a biological point of view, a 'drive' appears to us as a concept on the frontier between the mental and the somatic, as the psychical representative of the stimuli originating from within the organism and reaching the mind, as a measure of the demand made upon the mind for work in consequence of its connection with the body" (XIV:121–22). As a psychical representative, a drive does not *reach* the mind, as though it were coming from the outside, nor does it make a demand *upon* it, as though it were a barbarian pounding at the gate for admission. See Loewald, "On Motivation and Instinct Theory" and "Instinct Theory, Object Relations and Psychic Structure," in *Papers on Psychoanalysis*.

4. This is what Freud might have meant by "the drive in itself." If so, he seems to be giving pride of place to biology.

with two different things, but with two different ways in which the same thing is considered. This allows us to grant that a *drive* is a frontier creature, while allowing us to work with *concepts* that fall on one side of the frontier or the other. Since we are engaged in a psychological inquiry, the concept with which we wish to work is the drive considered psychologically: the psychic representative of biological stimuli and processes. We may, for convenience and brevity, simply call it a drive. That is the concept with which we are concerned. But then, when we say that a drive is the psychic representative of biological stimuli, there is no need to assume that the drive is a different thing from the biological stimuli it represents. The psychic representative and the biological stimuli it represents may be identical. That is, a drive might represent itself. The distinction between a drive and the biological stimuli it represents is essentially an *epistemological distinction*—marking a boundary in the way things are studied. It may or may not distinguish items in reality.[5]

A number of psychoanalytic thinkers have pointed out that the English word "instinct" has been used to translate two distinct concepts in Freud—that of *Instinkt* and of *Trieb*.[6] An *Instinkt*, for Freud, is a rigid, innate behavioral

---

5. That is, it may or may not mark a metaphysical distinction. (Analysts, if they use the word "metaphysics" at all, generally use it as a synonym for "nonsense." This is an unfortunate legacy of an outworn positivism: a positivism which, ironically, treated psychoanalysis as "nonsense." Metaphysics should be understood as the study of the broad-scale features of reality.) Freud, by the way, would have thought that there must be a metaphysical distinction between a psychical representative and that which it represents. For he treated consciousness on the model of perception. On this model, a distinct object would be causing awareness of it. But there is no inherent reason for thinking that this is the appropriate model of consciousness of inner states, so there is no inherent reason for thinking that a psychical representative cannot be identical with that which it represents.

6. See, e.g., Laplanche, *Life and Death in Psychoanalysis*, pp. 9–11; Bettelheim, *Freud and Man's Soul*, pp. 103–12.

pattern, characteristic of animal behavior: e.g., the innate ability and pressure of a bird to build a nest. It is the essence of an *Instinkt* that it could not have a vicissitude: the pattern of behavior that it fuels and directs is preformed and fixed. A *Trieb*, by contrast, has a certain plasticity: its aim and direction is to some extent shaped by experience. To conceive of humans as powered by *Triebe*, as Freud did, is in part to distinguish humanity from the rest of the animal world. I am not going to discuss the *Instinkt* at all. So whenever I speak of "the drives" or of "instinctual life," I am referring to *Triebe*.

Drives are a continuous source of pressure within human life. And this pressure has a distinctively psychological aspect. The meaning of a drive, therefore, is not given merely by its functional role within the organism. Since it is a psychical representative of biological stimuli, its meaning is given by the mental representation which partially constitutes it. Drives are the simplest constituents of the mind. Yet Freud's first attempt to formulate a theory of drives is very much one formulated from the outside.

> What distinguishes the drives from one another and endows them with specific qualities is their relation to their somatic sources and to their aims. The source of a drive is a process of excitation occurring in an organ and the immediate aim of the drive lies in the removal of this organic stimulus.[7]

The idea that drives are distinguished by their somatic sources is a red herring. Freud knew that it was beyond the scope of then current knowledge to isolate the physio-

---

7. *Three Essays on the Theory of Sexuality*, VII:168.

logical source of the drives. So whatever distinctions were to be made among the drives had to be made in ignorance of their sources. But, more importantly, the concept of drive, as it is used in psychoanalysis, should be a distinctively psychological concept. In formulating psychoanalysis as a distinctive realm of inquiry, Freud decided to theorize about the human being in abstraction from his physiological makeup. So if the drive cannot be characterized in psychological terms, it loses its claim to be a psychological concept. Freud implicitly acknowledges this. For though he assumes that there are two chemical forms of excitation arising in somatic organs, he admits in a footnote that it is not easy to justify this assumption, derived as it is from the study of neurosis.[8] He thus admits that his physiological hypothesis is based on psychological observation.

II

In practice, drives are distinguished by their aims. Freud defines the aim as the act toward which the drive tends.[9]

8. *Three Essays on the Theory of Sexuality*, VII:168–69 n. Cp. 243: "we know far too little of the biological processes constituting the essence of sexuality to construct a theory of both normal and pathological conditions." And see also, e.g., "The Unconscious," XIV:174–75: ". . . every attempt . . . to discover a localization of mental processes, every endeavour to think of ideas as stored up in nerve-cells and of excitations as travelling along nerve-fibres, has miscarried completely. The same fate would await any theory which attempted to recognize, let us say, the anatomical position of the system *Cs.*—conscious mental activity—as being in the cortex, and to localize the unconscious processes in the subcortical parts of the brain. There is a hiatus here which at present cannot be filled, nor is it one of the tasks of psychology to fill it. Our psychical topography has *for the present* nothing to do with anatomy; it has reference not to anatomical localities, but to regions in the mental apparatus, wherever they may be situated in the body. In this respect, then, our work is untrammelled and may proceed according to its own requirements."
9. *Three Essays on the Theory of Sexuality*, VII:136.

The drives are thus distinguished by what they are drives *for*. So if a drive is to be singled out and categorized as a sexual drive, it must be because of what that drive is striving toward. When Freud first introduced the sexual drive, it was by analogy with hunger, the drive for nutrition.[10] But why consider hunger a drive *for nutrition*? One cannot answer this question without a conception of a well-functioning animal. In beings who had no need to metabolize food, hunger might be a drive to fill the stomach or to transform vegetables into manure. Hunger is conceptualized as a drive for nutrition because we understand that in a well-functioning animal, the point of hunger is to motivate the animal to provide nourishment for himself.[11] By the same token, there is no basis for considering the drive Freud isolated a *sexual* drive unless that is the best way of understanding how that drive fits into the life of the well-functioning human being.

Freud realized this. At the beginning of his theorizing, the sexual drive seemed to count as sexual because it is expressed in or through parts of the body; because satisfying the drive regularly results in bodily pleasures; because in normal development the strivings for satisfaction through these parts of the body are subordinated to a striving for satisfaction through the genitals; and because in normal development this striving is subordinated to sexual repro-

---

10. *Three Essays on the Theory of Sexuality*, VII:135.

11. This is what Aristotle called a teleological explanation: an explanation in terms of the point, goal or *telos* of a certain activity. Although teleological explanations are used regularly throughout science, they are in unfairly bad repute. For it is often thought that a teleological explanation demands that the not yet existing goal of a process must mysteriously exert a backward-running causal influence. This is an absurd notion. It is also a straw man—a travesty of the concept. The traditional concept of teleological explanation had no such absurd consequence. See Aristotle, *Physics*, II. I discuss this in *Aristotle: The Desire to Understand*.

duction.[12] But Freud was quick to add a point to this sexual striving:

> The individual does actually carry on a twofold existence: one to serve his own purposes and the other as a link in a chain, which he serves against his will, or at least involuntarily. The individual himself regards sexuality as one of his own ends; whereas from another point of view he is an appendage to his germ-plasm, at whose disposal he puts his energies in return for a bonus of pleasure. He is the mortal vehicle of a (possibly) immortal substance—like the inheritor of an entailed property, who is only the temporary holder of an estate which survives him. The separation of the sexual drives from the I-drives would simply reflect this twofold function of the individual.[13]

The sexual drive is distinguished by its end, or goal. Unlike the I-drives, which function to preserve the individual, the sexual drive functions to preserve the species.

Now, the value of this type of reasoning is that it offers a picture of the overall functioning of the human being. It gives us a conception of what human sexuality is for. The occupational hazard of such reasoning, though, is that one will not correctly grasp the true point of, say, human sexuality. And Freud is himself quite clear that he is putting forward a hypothesis. But if the hypothesis is wrong, it is

---

12. *Three Essays on the Theory of Sexuality*; see esp. VII:207.

13. "On Narcissism: An Introduction" (1914), XIV:78. (I use "I-drives" and "sexual drives" where the Standard Edition uses "ego-instinct" and "sexual instincts," respectively.) Cp. "Instincts and Their Vicissitudes," XIV:125, and *Introductory Lectures*, XVI:412–14; and cp. Diotima's remark in Plato's *Symposium*: "And why all this longing for propagation? Because this is the one deathless and eternal element in our mortality" (206e).

not just that we will have misunderstood what sexuality is for; the very idea that it is sexuality that we are most basically concerned with may be called into question. For the sexual drive is being isolated as a *sexual* drive via its *aim*. If our conception of the aim changes, so might our conception of the drive we are trying to understand.

When Freud introduces the sexual drive in *Three Essays on the Theory of Sexuality*, he characterizes its aim from an observational stance. At the beginning of life, there is nothing observable that would lead one to posit a sexual drive. We can observe that the baby's sucking at the mother's breast is sensually pleasurable, but that observation alone only provides evidence that the satisfaction of the drives for self-preservation is pleasurable.[14] It is because the sexual drive detaches itself from the self-preservative drives that Freud is able so to conceptualize it.

The phenomenon that attracted his attention was thumb-sucking. Thumb-sucking, Freud argued, is an infantile attempt to re-create the pleasurable situation of being at the breast. But there is one aspect of being at the breast that is necessarily omitted from the re-creation. Thumb-sucking cannot be occurring for the purpose of self-preservation. The aim of the re-creation must differ from the aim of the prototypical act. One of the virtues of thumb-sucking is that the child, as it were, compensates himself for the independence and repeated absence of the maternal breast. Thumb-sucking is something he can do all by himself. Thus Freud called it "auto-erotic," a hallmark of infantile sexuality.[15] But to say that thumb-sucking is "auto-erotic" is, within

---

14. *Three Essays on the Theory of Sexuality*, VII:181–82.
15. *Three Essays on the Theory of Sexuality*, VII:182–83. The other hallmarks Freud mentions here are that infantile sexuality is derivative of one of the vital somatic functions and that its sexual aim is dominated by an erotogenic zone.

the context of *Three Essays*, only to say that a child sucks his own thumb. Freud defines the sexual object as the person (or thing) from whom sexual attraction proceeds.[16] So to say that infantile sexuality is "auto-erotic" is to characterize it from an external point of view, in abstraction from the psychic significance it has for the infant. This is a deficient way to characterize a drive, for it gives us no clue as to the mental representation which constitutes the drive.

Freud does discuss the psychological significance of infantile sexual activity. While feeding at the breast consists in the physical incorporation of nourishment, the sexual activity consists in the psychological incorporation of the sexual object.[17] That is, the child experiences feeding as a taking in of the breast, the mother, the mother's comfort. In latency, the child gives up the mother as an explicitly sexual object, and its sexual activity becomes "auto-erotic." But when, in puberty, the child again begins to look for a sexual object, the psychological impact of the mother makes itself manifest.

There are . . . good reasons why a child sucking at his mother's breast has become the prototype of every relation of love. The finding of an object is in fact a refinding of it.[18]

---

16. *Three Essays on the Theory of Sexuality*, VII:135–36.

17. See *Three Essays on the Theory of Sexuality*, VII:198. Freud puts this point misleadingly when he says that the object of both activities is the same. In anal erotism, to give a second example, the sexual instinct detaches itself from a biological function. It becomes pleasurable for the child to hold back stools and then let them explode. The stools, says Freud, are treated by the child as part of his own body and are given as a gift. They are also used as a means of demonstrating compliance or disobedience. Later on, the evacuation of bowels comes to represent an act of birth and the stools come to signify babies in infantile theories of sexuality. (VII:185–86.)

18. *Three Essays on the Theory of Sexuality*, VII:222.

This refinding is not a purely physiological process, as when the leaves of a plant "refind" the sun. Freud's point is that no matter how distinctive a later love relation may appear, for the persons involved there will be psychic resonances with the earliest, most primitive emotional-sexual bond. The very possibility of these resonances depends upon the mother's breast having had a significance for the infant. Thus it is a mistake to characterize the object of a drive solely from an external point of view. The earliest object of the sexual drive cannot be the mother's breast *tout court*; it must be the mother's breast as psychologically experienced by the infant. This sheds light on the plasticity of the sexual drive. For while the sexual drive does exercise a constraining influence on our choices—there is a psychologically signif- icant sense in which our later overtly sexual choices are "like" our earlier infantile sexual objects—the fact that our first sexual object, the breast, has been psychologically me- tabolized allows it to be subject to archaic and higher-level mental activity. And this allows the possibility of "refinding the breast" in something other than a breast. Every "re- finding" may also be a discovery.

Now, when Freud in *Three Essays* calls the child's thumb- sucking "auto-erotic," he conceptualizes the infantile sexual drive independently of its psychic significance. And yet if the "auto-erotic" is to be erotic, one must see the "auto" as a mere façade.[19] It is because Freud looks at the variety of sexual objects from the outside that he is able to reach the following conclusion:

> It has been brought to our notice that we have been
> in the habit of regarding the connection between the

---

19. Once one takes the psychic significance of an activity into account one sees that, *contra* Woody Allen, masturbation is not something one can do all by oneself.

sexual drive and the sexual object as more intimate than it in fact is. Experience of the cases that are considered abnormal has shown us that in them the sexual drive and the sexual object are merely *soldered together*—a fact which we have been in danger of overlooking in consequence of the uniformity of the normal picture, where the object appears to form part and parcel of the drive. We are thus warned to loosen the bond that exists in our thoughts between drive and object. It seems probable that the sexual drive is in the first instance independent of its object; nor is its origin likely to be due to the object's attractions.[20]

This is not the first time Freud has used the metaphor of soldering. In his discussion of dreams, he says that an an idea and the emotion attaching to it are merely soldered together.[21] What he meant was that an emotion can be detached from the idea to which it is appropriate and then be attached to any idea whatever. However, as we have seen, this detachment only occurs at the manifest level of consciousness. Once we consider the deeper, latent content of a dream, it emerges that an emotion is indissolubly attached to its appropriate idea. Similarly with the sexual drive and the sexual object. It is because the sexual object is considered solely at the manifest level of casual observation that it appears merely soldered to the sexual drive.

Once one defines a sexual object in terms of its psychological significance, the lesson of *Three Essays* seems to be the opposite of what Freud says it is. There is a sense in which the sexual drive never abandons its object. The succession of sexual objects follows the loose associations of

---

20. *Three Essays on the Theory of Sexuality*, VII:147–48 (my emphasis).
21. *The Interpretation of Dreams*, V:462. See Chapter 3 above.

archaic mental functioning.²² And thus it is only from the
perspective of secondary-process thinking that the succession appears a succession. From the perspective of archaic
mind, there may be no significant difference among these
"different" objects. By ignoring the sexual object's psychological significance, one cuts the drive loose from the moor-
ings that give it meaning. And by taking an observational
stance, one ironically deprives the external world of its significance. The world then presents itself as eminently detachable: of no deep significance to the fickle human. What
the observational stance cannot see is that in all his wan-
dering among sexual objects, there is a sense in which the
person has never left home. By ignoring the internal world,
one impoverishes the external world. Thus both worlds lose
significance.

III

Freud speculates that "the sexual drive is in the first instance
independent of its object." This seems odd, given that the
infant is from birth sucking at the breast. But Freud's speculation is not based on infant observation. It probably arose
from his attempt to make sense of psychosis. Although he
confronted psychosis in adults, there were two prominent
clinical phenomena which, he thought, shed light on infantile mental life: a typical fantasy of world catastrophe and
megalomania.²³ Freud thinks these phenomena are related.
The fantasy of world destruction is, Freud hypothesizes, a

22. See, e.g., "A Special Type of Choice of Object Made by Men," XI:165 ff.
23. See, for example, Freud's account of the Senatspräsident Schreber in
"Psycho-Analytic Notes on an Autobiographical Account of a Case of Paranoia,"
XII:69–79; "On Narcissism: An Introduction," XIV:74–76.

psychotic representation of a real process: a person's withdrawal of interest from the external world.[24] For Freud, a person's interest in the world is a manifestation of his investing it with sexual energy, which he called *libido*. The world's ceasing to exist for a person and his withdrawal of libido from the world are, for Freud, two aspects of the same process. What it is like for the person is that the world ceases to exist: this is his psychological representation. The withdrawal of libido is what is really happening.

What has happened to the withdrawn libido? It has, Freud speculates, filled up the I, giving the person a sense of omnipotent power, magical ability, specialness. This is the megalomania. Freud noticed a family resemblance between the psychotic's megalomania and the magical thinking of children, and inferred that psychotic megalomania was not just a withdrawal of libido from objects, but a *regression* to an infantile form of mentality. He hypothesized that the original psychical situation was one of libido bound up and contained within the I.

> Thus we form the idea of there being an original libidinal investment of the I, from which some is later given off to objects, but which fundamentally persists and is related to the object-investments much as the body of an amoeba is related to the pseudo-podia it puts out.[25]

Here Freud is too much under the sway of a biological model. The newborn baby is a biological individual. And if there is a physiological basis for sexual energy, it will be

---

24. The end of the world (for the psychotic) is (from a psychoanalytic point of view) the psychotic's withdrawal of interest in that world.
25. "On Narcissism," XIV:75.

physically located within the biological individual. But, psychologically speaking, an individual does not yet exist. There is no I yet on the scene: at best there is a proto-I, an archaic precursor from which, in good-enough circumstances, an I will emerge.[26] For this proto-I, there are no firm boundaries between inside and outside, no firm boundaries between self and other. Indeed, there is no established sense of self, and so experience permeates a less differentiated field. Given this primitive mental state, there can be no content to the idea of an original libidinal investment of the I. Nor can the I send out libido like pseudo-podia. In the psychological world of the newly born infant, there is not yet a firmly established inside from which libido can be sent out; nor is there yet an outside to which libido can be sent.[27]

The sexual drive is a psychological force. For a person to be able libidinally to invest in an object, the object must be something *for* the person. The object must have psychic reality. This must be true even when that "object" is the I or the self. Freud is speculating that psychotic megalomania is a regression to an original psychological state. But for that original state to be anything like megalomania, it cannot be merely that a physiological substrate for libido is in the biological individual. That will be true whether a person invests in objects or the self. Megalomania must be a libidinal *investment* of the I. And for that to be possible, the I must represent itself. That is, the I must have psychological reality for itself. It can no longer uncritically be taken to be the biological individual in whom and around whom various

---

26. I discuss the proto-I further in the next chapter.

27. See Loewald, "Ego and Reality," in *Papers on Psychoanalysis*; Laplanche, *Life and Death in Psychoanalysis*, Chapter 4; Winnicott, "The Depressive Position in Normal Emotional Development," in *Through Paediatrics to Psycho-Analysis*; Mahler, *The Psychological Birth of the Human Infant*, pp. 41–50; Kohut, *The Analysis of the Self*, pp. 19, 33, 42, 90.

psychological dramas occur. The I must itself be within the domain of the psychological. What Freud is beginning to realize is that part of what it is to be an I is to have a self-representation, which is itself invested with one's own libido. As he says, "a unity comparable to the I cannot exist in the individual from the start." "A new psychical action" is needed, Freud says, in order for narcissism, the libidinal investment of the I, to be possible.[28] This new psychical action is the formation of the I as a psychological entity. It is not there at the beginning. It is not just that the infant doesn't realize that he is an individual: part of what it is to be an individual is to recognize oneself to be one.[29] So it is only from a third-personal, biological point of view that one could be tempted to think that there is an individual there to be a reservoir of libido.

If we try to capture the psychological world of the infant, we have to say that there is not yet any I to invest; nor is there a distinct world of objects for which there could be a possible question of extending or withholding libido. For the infant, there are no firm boundaries between subject and object, and thus there is (for him) no subject and no object. Nor are there firm boundaries between inner and outer, and thus there is (for him) no inner and outer. These distinctions are all psychological achievements. And insofar as drives are psychological, *internal* sources of pressure, we have to say that at this earliest stage, the drives do not yet

---

28. "On Narcissism," XIV:77.

29. Of course, this self-recognition may be rudimentary, and it will differ from the I's ability to recognize any other object in the world. In part, the I is presented to itself in its proprioceptive sense of its own limbs, its muscular power, its non-discursive knowledge of what it intends to do, its perceptual perspective on the world. Thus the I's self-representation need not be from a sideways-on perspective. The point is only that the I must have a psychological awareness of itself as a unity. We do not yet understand all that is involved in the experience of such unity, so we do not yet fully understand what the I's "self-representation" consists in. For a fascinating discussion of this, see Brian O'Shaughnessy, *The Will*.

exist either.[30] They are in the process of formation. So "primary narcissism," the original psychic state, ought to be understood as libidinal investment that permeates a relatively undifferentiated field: a field from which an I and a distinct world for that I will emerge.

Freud at least experimented with this alternative conception of primary narcissism. In *Civilization and Its Discontents*, he tries to explain the "oceanic" feeling of being at one with the world and the feelings of lovers that the boundaries between them "threaten to melt away."[31] Freud speculated that this feeling of merging was a regression to an early form of psychic experience where there was no firm boundary between self and other.

> . . . the adult's I-feeling cannot have been the same from the beginning. It must have gone through a process of development, which cannot, of course, be demonstrated but which admits of being constructed with a fair degree of probability. An infant at the breast does not as yet distinguish his I from the external world as the source of the sensations flowing in upon him. He gradually learns to do so, in response to various promptings. . . . In this way there is for the first time set over against the I an "object," in the form of something which exists "outside" and which is only forced to appear by a special action.[32]

This original psychic state establishes within the adult a permanent possibility of regression. The oceanic feeling is,

---

30. See Loewald, "On Motivation and Instinct Theory" and "Instinct Theory, Object Relations and Psychic Structure," in *Papers on Psychoanalysis*.
31. *Civilization and Its Discontents*, XXI:64–73.
32. *Civilization and Its Discontents*, XXI:66–67.

Freud speculated, a psychic return to a state prior to the differentiation of an I from the world.

A concern with sexuality has forced psychoanalysis to become philosophical. For once psychoanalysis sees that the I is a psychological achievement—that it is not just there from the beginning—it cannot help but ask what that achievement consists in. Although Freud had been speaking of the I since *Studies on Hysteria*, the concept of the I was more or less taken for granted. In *Studies*, the I is said to be "the dominant mass of ideas" with which a desire comes into conflict and is cast out.[33] And although Freud's unfolding research has revealed ever more about what it is to be an I, the concept of an I has been left out of account. It is only when Freud realizes that an I can be the object of its own sexual investment that the concept of an I becomes a focus of psychoanalytic attention.[34]

Neither can psychoanalysis any longer take the nature of the world for granted. For it is constitutive of the process of an I coming into being that there comes to be a world of objects for that I. It is a single process by which an I and a world of objects come to be differentiated out of the undifferentiated psychic field that we call "primary narcissism." And if the psychotic's end of the world is in fact a withdrawal of libido, this suggests that a world exists for us because we invest it with sexual energy. Of course, we do not think that the world of objects *really* comes into being with this "new psychical action." At most, what we mean is that the world of objects, which, after all, really

33. *Studies on Hysteria*, II:116.
34. And what Freud discovers is that the process by which the I is formed is fueled by sexual energy, and that it is sexual energy that holds the I together. I shall discuss this in the next chapter.

exists, comes to have psychic reality for this emerging I.[35]
When we talk about the *psychological world* of the psychotic
or the psychological world of the infant we are trying to
capture the subjectivity of the being whose psychological
world it is. We are trying to determine what it is like, say,
to be an infant. Here we are trying to capture the quality
of the infant's fantasy life and his ever-increasing appreciation of self and reality. But in the same breath we distance
ourselves both from his subjectivity and from his world. It
is easy to see this in the case of the world. For one of the
points in insisting upon its being *the psychological world of*
the infant is to make it clear that we do not think that this
is the way the world really is. We are signaling an important
gap between the infant's subjective appreciation of the
world, on the one hand, and the world as it objectively is,
on the other.

But what is the philosophical content of the world really
being some way? When we talk of the objective world, are
we not talking about the world as it appears to mature,
scientific investigators with adult consciousness? That is,
the contrast between the psychological world of X and the
world as it really is is not a contrast between X's subjectivity
and some unknowable world-as-it-is-in-itself. It is, rather,
a contrast between X's subjectivity and the world as it is

35. It might thus reasonably appear that the sexual drive is more deeply involved in the constitution of the I than it is in the constitution of the world. To
give one example: when we say that the world ceases to exist for the psychotic,
we do not think that the world *really* ceases to exist. We are trying to capture
the psychotic's psychological world: that it is for him as though there were no
external world. By contrast, if the libidinal bonds constituting and holding the
psychotic's mind truly give out, we do not say that the psychotic's mind ceases
to exist for the psychotic (but it continues to exist really). The situation we are
trying to capture is not: it is for the psychotic as though he didn't have a mind.
We are trying to capture the idea that it is not for him like anything—he is no
longer even psychotic—for there is no longer any mind in virtue of which it could
be for him like something (or other).

knowable and appreciated *by us*. When we are talking about the real world, the "by us" cancels out.[36] However, in philosophical reflection we realize that the real world is a world we appreciate and (after due consideration) take to be objective. This is not meant to diminish the objectivity of the objective world: it is merely to remind us that the objective world, to be the objective world that it is, must be an objective world *for us*.

Reflection on the psychotic's end of the world reveals that the world exists *for us* because we invest it with sexual energy. So far, the "because" seems straightforwardly causal: we libidinally invest the world and it comes to have reality for us. Were we to withdraw libidinal investment in the world, it would come to an end (for us). So at most what would happen is that the world would go out of existence *for us*, but in fact the world would continue to be. So the thought goes. And it is a compelling thought, for we tend to think of the world as something that is there *anyway*, independent of our thinking or of our interest in it.

And yet, we have already acknowledged that the real world must in some sense be the world as it appears to us. So in conceiving of the real world as continuing to exist as we fall apart, what we are conceiving is the world as it *would* appear to beings like us (were there any such beings). But Freud's point is that sexuality so pervades us, so pervades the way we see and understand things, that the world as it would appear to beings like us must be a world which is a fit object of sexual investment by beings like us. That is the world that is there anyway.

To see this, consider the claim:

---

36. See my paper "The Disappearing 'We.' "

The world exists because we invest it with sexual energy.

Or, to shed the last remnants of jargon:

The world exists because we love it.

Freud sanctioned this transition himself. In *Group Psychology and the Analysis of the Ego*, he introduces the concept of sexual energy as follows:

Libido is an expression taken from the theory of the emotions. We call by that name the energy, regarded as a quantitative magnitude (though not at present actually measurable), of those instincts which have to do with all that may be comprised under the word "love." The nucleus of what we mean by love naturally consists (and this is what is commonly called love, and what the poets sing of) in sexual love with sexual union as its aim. But we do not separate from this—what in any case has a share in the name "love"—on the one hand, self-love, and on the other, love for parents and children, friendship and love for humanity in general, and also devotion to concrete objects and to abstract ideas. Our justification lies in the fact that psychoanalytic research has taught us that all these tendencies are an expression of the same instinctual impulses; in relations between the sexes these impulses force their way towards sexual union, but in other circumstances they are diverted from this aim or are prevented from reaching it, though always preserving enough of their original nature to keep their identity recognizable . . .
   We are of the opinion, then, that language has car-

ried out an entirely justifiable piece of unification in creating the word "love" with its numerous uses, and that we cannot do better than take it as the basis of our scientific discussions and expositions as well. By coming to this decision, psycho-analysis has let loose a storm of indignation, as though it had been guilty of an act of outrageous innovation. Yet it has done nothing original in taking love in this "wider" sense. In its origin, function, and relation to sexual love, the "Eros" of the philosopher Plato coincides exactly with the love-force, the libido of psycho-analysis . . .[37]

Now, when we come to consider a statement like:

The world exists because we love it

it is not at all clear how to understand it. Both the meaning of this statement and its truth or falsity depend on how we interpret the "because." If we treat the "because" as straight-forwardly causal, then the statement seems to say that the world comes into existence due to our investing it with sexual energy. This is false. The world exists *anyway*, whether or not we come to appreciate its existence. And yet we cannot just wash our hands of the matter. There seems to be a deeper interpretation of the claim which cannot be so tidily dismissed. To work toward a philosophical understanding of this claim, it would seem that we need to interpret the "because" thus:

---

37. *Group Psychology and the Analysis of the Ego*, XVIII:90–92. See also his discussion of Grabbe's remark, "We cannot fall out of this world," in *Civilization and Its Discontents*, XXI:65 f.

It is a condition of there being a world that it be lovable by beings like us.

That the world need only be lov*able* frees the world's existence from any causal dependence on our actually loving it.[38] The world does not exist because it is actually loved—or invested with libido—but it is a condition of there being a world that it be lovable by beings like us. This is more than a psychological condition of there being a world *for us*. There is no content to the idea of a world that is not a possible world for us. And a world that is not lovable (by beings like us) is not a possible world.

IV

Now, when we say that the world must be lovable, it may seem that we have traveled a long way from sex, but Freud's own thinking followed a similar trajectory. What it was for the sexual drive to be a *sexual* drive was a continuing concern for Freud, and the more he thought about it, the more the sexual drive expanded to impregnate the world.

But before tracing the similarity of the trajectory, I would like to point out one important difference. Freud was, by his own admission, a speculative thinker. On the basis of the clinical phenomena he observed, he would speculate as to the general principles at work in nature. That is, he would treat the clinical phenomenon as though it were the conclusion of an argument and try to work *backward* to the "premises" from which the "conclusion" was derived.[39]

---

38. Or hating it.
39. This is analysis in the sense of ancient Greek geometry.

Freud was in this sense a *speculative* metaphysician. Of course, working in this direction involves a certain amount of guesswork, and Freud always gave pride of place to the clinical phenomena on which his speculations were based. The speculations were, for him, superstructure; and he repeatedly expressed a willingness to modify them in the light of new clinical experience or a better conceptualization.[40] Nevertheless, he did respect the activity of speculation and he admired great speculative thinkers.[41] The approach I have been taking, by contrast, is not speculative in this sense. I have been inquiring what the world must be like, given the psychoanalytic understanding of human existence. The inquiry is into the conditions of the possibility of psychoanalysis. Or, rather, it is an inquiry into the conditions of the possibility of human existence (given the psychoanalytic understanding of what it is to be human). It is *internal* metaphysics because it is working within the concepts of psychoanalysis, trying to deduce their metaphysical implications.[42] It treats the clinical phenomena as "premises" and works *forward* toward metaphysical "conclusions." This ap-

---

40. See, e.g., "On Narcissism: An Introduction," XIV:79; *The Ego and the Id*, XIX:42; *Beyond the Pleasure Principle*, XVIII:44, 59–60.

41. See, e.g., Freud's remarks on Empedocles: "His mind seems to have united the sharpest contrasts. He was exact and sober in his physical and physiological researches, yet he did not shrink from the obscurities of mysticism, and built up cosmic speculations of astonishingly imaginative boldness"; ". . . no one can foresee in what guise the nucleus of truth contained in the theory of Empedocles will present itself to later understanding." ("Analysis Terminable and Interminable," XXIII:245, 247.) And after introducing the idea of a battle between erotic and death drives in *New Introductory Lectures on Psycho-Analysis*, Freud says, "You may perhaps shrug your shoulders and say: 'That isn't natural science, it's Schopenhauer's philosophy!' But, ladies and gentlemen, why should not a bold thinker have guessed something that is afterwards confirmed by sober and painstaking detailed research?" (XXII:107.)

42. This bears a resemblance to what Kant called a transcendental investigation; the main difference being that this inquiry is not carried out a priori or independently of experience. See *Critique of Pure Reason*, Bxiv–xxiv.

proach is less free-ranging than some of Freud's daring speculations, but it does allow us to pursue the hidden implications of the clinical phenomena.

Now, when Freud first introduced the sexual drive, he treated the distinction between the sexual drive and the I-drive as straightforward. But this distinction must be called into question by his discovery of narcissism: that sexual energy can invest the normal workings of the I, that it can invest normal bodily functions. Freud isolated the sexual drive when it *detached* itself from the I-drive of hunger and manifested itself in auto-erotic thumb-sucking. With the introduction of narcissism, Freud is in a position to see that the sexual drive can *reattach* itself to the I-drive.[43] Even if what we take into our mouth is nourishing, it may also have sexual significance. And this must raise the issue of whether the sexual drive ever really left. That is, what basis remains for thinking there are two classes of drives? Perhaps all the so-called drives are fueled by sexual energy and thus all count as manifestations of the sexual drive. Or, perhaps, sexual energy is not at bottom sexual energy: that is, perhaps sexuality is a manifestation of a more fundamental force permeating nature. After all, once Freud discovered that the sexual drive can invest normal I-functions and thus exist in a "desexualized" form, the question must arise as to whether the sexual drive is best conceived of as a distinctively sexual drive.

To answer this challenge, Freud violated his "other" fun-

---

43. A reader of the English translation, "On Narcissism: An Introduction," might be forgiven for thinking that Freud's aim is to introduce him to the concept of narcissism. A more literal translation of the title, "Zur Einführung des Narzissmus," would make it clear that Freud's aim is to introduce narcissism into psychoanalytic theory.

damental rule.[44] That is, he was committed to providing psychological explanations of the phenomena and to formulating theoretical principles on the basis of these explanations. He recognized that science may one day also provide a biological explanation of the very phenomena which he had explained psychoanalytically, but the viability of psychoanalysis as a distinctive and unified discipline depended on his being able to give a peculiarly psychoanalytical explanation. In that sense, psychoanalysis had to be self-contained, even if it welcomed another, biological level of explanation. But with the introduction of narcissism, Freud felt he had to go outside.

> I try in general to keep psychology clear from everything that is different in nature from it, even biological lines of thought. For that very reason I should like at this point expressly to admit that the hypothesis of separate I-drives and sexual drives (that is to say, the libido theory) rests scarcely at all upon a psychological basis, but derives its principal support from biology.[45]

The ultimate point in turning to biology, though, was not to preserve the I-drives per se, but to preserve a Something Else that was in conflict with the sexual drive. For by the time Freud wrote *Beyond the Pleasure Principle* in 1920, he was willing to abandon the fundamental opposition between the sexual drive and the I-drive, but only to substitute another for it. The sexual drive was "transformed" into Eros, the love or life drive, and the new Something Else is the

---

44. The famous fundamental rule is, of course, that the analysand be instructed to say whatever comes into his mind without censorship. I began to discuss this in Chapter 1.
45. "On Narcissism: An Introduction," XIV:78–79.

death drive, a force in every living cell for decomposition and return to an inorganic state. Again Freud's argument for this Something Else is, as he is well aware, grounded in biological speculation.[46] And he admits that from within a strictly psychoanalytical perspective, one can only see the sexual drive at work.[47] Of course, Freud thinks that sadism and aggression, which one can see, are manifestations of the death drive turned outward. But it is only because he has *already* posited a death drive that he can see aggression as a deflected instance of it. Within the organism, the death drive "remains silent."[48]

The fundamental nature of conflict within human life, Freud thought, must reflect a conflict of fundamental forces. It was never acceptable to him that human conflict should be founded on the (perhaps inevitable) vicissitudes of sexuality alone. There had to be Something Else with which sexuality was struggling.[49] But when the Something Else

---

46. Cp., e.g., *Beyond the Pleasure Principle*, XVIII:37–61; *The Ego and the Id*, XIX:40; "Two Encyclopedia Articles," XVIII:258.

47. *Beyond the Pleasure Principle*, XVIII:52–53.

48. *An Outline of Psycho-Analysis*, XXIII:150: "So long as [the destructive] instinct operates internally, *as a death instinct, it remains silent*; it only comes to our notice when it is diverted outwards as an instinct of destruction." And cp. *Beyond the Pleasure Principle*, XVIII:59–60; "Two Encyclopedia Articles," XVIII:258; "An Autobiographical Study," XX:57. See also *The Ego and the Id*, XIX:46: "Over and over again we find, when we are able to trace drive impulses back, that they reveal themselves as derivatives of Eros. If it were not for the considerations put forward in *Beyond the Pleasure Principle*, and ultimately for the sadistic constituents which have attached themselves to Eros, we should have difficulty in holding to our fundamental dualistic point of view. But since we cannot escape that view we are driven to conclude that *the death drives are by their nature mute* and that the clamour of life proceeds for the most part from Eros."

49. Thus Freud complained that charges of "pan-sexualism" were unfair, for "the psycho-analytic theory of the instincts had always been strictly dualistic and had at no time failed to recognize, alongside the sexual instincts, others to which it actually ascribed force enough to suppress the sexual instincts." ("Resistances to Psycho-Analysis," XIX:218.) Cp., e.g., *Beyond the Pleasure Principle*, XVIII:60–61 n.; *The Ego and the Id*, XIX:46, 42; and "Analysis Terminable and Interminable": "Only by the concurrent or mutually opposing action of the two

became the death drive, the sexual drive had to be reconceptualized. For the struggle now did not confine itself to the human soul; it was occurring throughout animate nature, even within a single living cell. The sexual drive was now no more than a manifestation within humans of a principle that permeated life. The sexual drive had, in short, become a cosmological principle and had to be so conceived.[50]

Sex thus metamorphosed into love. Freud knew that he was extending "the popular conception" of sexuality.[51] His aim, though, was not to get away from the body, its smells, feels and drives, but to understand in the deepest sense what these drives are. Human sexuality is an incarnation of love, a force for unification present wherever there is life. (I shall speak of "love" rather than "eros" to avoid the pitfall of using a non-English term to muffle the intensity of Freud's thought.) Without love, the living cell or organism would fall apart under the pressure of the death drive. From the newly won perspective of love, Freud could now see that

primal instincts—Eros and the death instinct—never by one or the other alone, can we explain the rich multiplicity of the phenomena of life." (XXIII:243, cp. 246.) Cp. "Why War?" XXII:209.

50. See, e.g., *The Ego and the Id*, XIX:41: "The problem of the origin of life would remain a cosmological one; and the problem of the goal and purpose of life would be answered dualistically." In "Analysis Terminable and Interminable," Freud says that Empedocles' theory of the universe being governed by two natural forces, love and strife, is "one which approximates so closely to the psychoanalytic theory of the drives that we should be tempted to maintain that the two are identical, if it were not for the difference that the Greek philosopher's theory is a cosmic fantasy, while ours is content to claim biological validity." But in case anyone should think he is denying cosmological status to the instincts, he continues: "At the same time, the fact that Empedocles ascribes to the universe the same animate nature as to individual organisms, robs this difference of much importance." (XXIII:245–46.)

51. See, e.g., "Why War?" XXII:209; the Preface to the fourth edition of *Three Essays on the Theory of Sexuality* (1920), VII:134; *Group Psychology and the Analysis of the Ego*, XVIII:90–92; *The Interpretation of Dreams*, footnote added in 1925, IV:161 n.; *Beyond the Pleasure Principle*, XVIII:50.

what he originally isolated as the sexual drive was only libido that invested objects.[52] In his treatment of pathologies of sexual experience, Freud happened onto a force which, as his research developed, expanded beyond anything one could easily recognize as sexual. But rather than abandon the concept of sexuality, he let his discoveries fill up the concept and give it content.[53] Libido, he now found, could invest both objects and the I. Indeed, sexual energy could even exist in a "desexualized" form, a unifying force holding the self together. "The enlarged sexuality of psychoanalysis," Freud says, "coincides with the love of the divine Plato."[54]

> . . . what psychoanalysis calls sexuality was by no means identical with the impulsion towards a union of the two sexes or towards producing a pleasurable sensation in the genitals; it had far more resemblance to the all-inclusive and all-embracing love of Plato's *Symposium*.[55]

In fact, Freud tells us little about love.[56] And if we look to the *Symposium*, we find there an idea which is implicit in Freud's emerging thought: that love pulls us in two direc-

---

52. *Beyond the Pleasure Principle*, XVIII:60 n.

53. *Group Psychology and the Analysis of the Ego*, XVIII:91.

54. Preface to the fourth edition of *Three Essays on the Theory of Sexuality* (1920), VII:134. See also *Beyond the Pleasure Principle*, XVIII:50; *Group Psychology and the Analysis of the Ego*, XVIII:91.

55. "Resistances to Psychoanalysis," XIX:218. For other references to Plato's *Symposium*, see "Why War?" XXII:209.

56. Cp. Loewald, *Sublimation*: "I cannot emphasize enough that it was the introduction of the idea of the life instinct (which encompassed different conceptions of pleasure and of the pleasure principle) that was a true and unsettling innovation in psychoanalytic theory—an innovation that Freud could no longer circumvent but with which he felt much less at home than he did with the death instinct . . ." (30).

tions. In Aristophanes' myth, love is a regressive force by which we yearn to reestablish a previously existing unity.[57] We are, according to this myth, descended from hermaphroditic creatures who were cut in half by Zeus. Love is a pressure within us to restore a lost unity. Aristophanes' love impels us to abolish the boundaries between individuals.

There is evidence that Freudian love pulls us in the same direction. Every finding, Freud says, is a refinding, but some findings are more like the original than others. Humans by nature develop. But there is also within us a tendency to return to earlier stages at which we have received gratification and love. That love may have been needed for the development to progress, but it also establishes an everpresent undertow. The sexual drive is, according to Freud, essentially conservative. In its attempt to preserve life it attempts to restore a past that was successfully lived and loved. In that sense, love is historically minded, and the unity that a person is thereby impelled to seek is with his own past. Given the nature of human development, the pressure to restore must be a pressure to regress: to move back to a less differentiated psychological organization. Freud was primarily concerned with the tendency to regress to a more primitive sexual organization. Here the differentiated unity of adult sexual organization splits apart, and what should be "component" drives, for, say, oral or anal gratification, come to dominate a person's life.

Freud does speculate that love aims to restore a lost unity with another. He explains the lovers' feeling that the boundaries between them are melting as a regression to an undifferentiated unity: ". . . originally the I includes

57. *Symposium*, 189–93.

everything, later it separates off an external world from itself. Our present I-feeling is, therefore, only a shrunken residue of a much more inclusive—indeed all-embracing— feeling which corresponded to a more intimate bond between the I and the world about it."[58] In fact, the original intimate bond is between an infant not-yet-I and a mother-world. In this state, two individuals do not yet exist.[59] Though Freud did not pursue the consequences of this insight, he recognizes love's pull toward the primitive. "Love," he says, "desires contact because it strives to make the I and the love object one, to abolish all spatial barriers between them."[60] And although Freud recognized that civilization is a differentiated unity held together by love, Freud also saw that there was an erotic tendency for society to regress to a primitive, undifferentiated mob.[61]

Love, however, also pulls us in the opposite direction. It fuels human development and pulls us toward higher, more differentiated unities.

> . . . the libidinal, sexual or life instincts . . . are best comprised under the name *love*; their purpose would be to form living substance into ever greater unities, so that life may be prolonged and brought to higher development.[62]

58. *Civilization and Its Discontents*, XXI:68.

59. As "Aristophanes" said, "all this to-do is a relic of that original state of ours, when we were whole, and now, when we are longing for and following after that primeval wholeness, we say we are in love." Plato, *Symposium* 193a.

60. *Inhibitions, Symptoms and Anxiety*, XX:122. Cp. Freud's Encyclopaedia Britannica entry on "Psychoanalysis," where he speaks of "Eros, the instinct which strives for ever closer union" (XX:265).

61. See *Group Psychology and the Analysis of the Ego*, esp. XVIII:91–92. I discuss this further in the next chapter.

62. "Two Encyclopedia Articles," XVIII:258. See also, e.g., *Outline of Psycho-Analysis*, XXIII:148; *New Introductory Lectures on Psycho-Analysis*, XXII:108; *Civilization and Its Discontents*, XXI:108; *The Ego and the Id*, XIX:45.

The model for this higher unity is the living organism, which depends for its existence on the differentiated functioning of its parts. Love, however, must be more than a brutely natural unifying force. When it is manifested in humans, love is also a psychological force. So there must be something that it is like for the human who is striving to unify. Of course, a person may only have a dim understanding of what he is trying to do, but if humanly incarnated love is a psychological force, there must be something that *he* is trying to do. Freud virtually ignores this first-personal aspect of the erotic drive for unification. For example, Freud was suspicious of the idea of a "drive towards perfection." The individual's striving toward perfection, the development of "all that is most precious in human civilization," can be understood, he argued, as the outcome of repression's blocking the backward-running path of regressive satisfaction. There is, he says, no other path along which to grow. He goes on to suggest that "the efforts of love to combine organic substances into ever larger unities probably provide a substitute for this 'drive towards perfection' whose existence we cannot admit."[63] Here Freud must be treating love as a brute organizing force: only thus could he invoke it to explain the "drive towards perfection" away. For if human love has a first-personal aspect, the drive for higher unities may well express itself within human life as a drive for perfection.

The "divine Plato" realized that one could not capture love within human life unless one understood what lovers are trying to do. What a lover wants, says Socrates' teacher Diotima, is to get hold of the good and possess it forever. It is the essence of human life that the lover's desire must

---

63. *Beyond the Pleasure Principle*, XVIII:42–43.

be frustrated. A human is not divine and not immortal. So propagating upon the beautiful, both in body and in soul, is the best effort mortal humans can make to achieve their immortal aim.[64] This is what lovers are trying to do.

"In its origin, function and relation to sexual love," Freud says, *"the 'love' of the philosopher Plato coincides exactly with the love-force, the libido of psychoanalysis."*[65] It is strange, then, that Freud did not try to capture the point of love within human life. All the more so since by the time he wrote "The Economic Problem of Masochism," in 1924, he realized that he could not capture the movements of libido in a mechanistic model. Freud there recognized that there are some buildups of tension, notably in sexual foreplay, that are pleasurable and some discharges that are unpleasurable, and he drew the conclusion that ultimately undermines his mechanistic model of the mind:

Pleasure and unpleasure, therefore, cannot be referred to an increase or decrease of a quantity. . . . It appears that they depend, not on this quantitative factor, but on some characteristic of it which we can only describe as a qualitative one. If we were able to say what this qualitative characteristic is, we should be much further advanced in psychology.[66]

Freud never pursued this qualitative factor. And yet, he provides us with the conceptual materials to do so. If libido is love, then the qualitative factor ought to be found in the

---

64. *Symposium*, 205–12.

65. *Group Psychology and the Analysis of the Ego*, XVIII:91 (my emphasis).

66. "The Economic Problem of Masochism," XIX:160. Cp. *The Ego and the Id*, XIX:44: "The problem of the quality of instinctual impulses and its persistence throughout their various vicissitudes is still very obscure and has hardly been attacked up to the present."

lover's experienced relation with the object of his love. In the most general case, as we have seen, a person is erotically bound to the world. That is a condition of there being a world for him: that is, it is a condition of his sanity. But if our tie to the world is genuinely erotic, we can no longer conceive the world as a mere receiver or inhibitor of our discharges. Love is not just a feeling or a discharge of energy, but an emotional orientation to the world. That orientation demands that the world present itself to us as worthy of our love.[67] That is what it is for the world to be lovable. So far, we are working at a very abstract level. We don't yet know what it is about the world that, in our eyes, justifies our love. But it is plausible to suppose that *that* is the qualitative factor that needs to be captured. Whatever its regressive tendencies, love is also a force within us for development into an ever more complex and higher unity. The world must now be conceived as, at least potentially, providing an occasion for that development. By the same token, the mind operating according to the reality principle can no longer be seen as a mere detour or deferred satisfaction of instincts operating according to the pleasure principle.[68] It is via a certain type of erotic relation with the world that this development can take place.

What type of relation is this? Freud does give us a hint.

---

67. See above, pages 47–51.

68. Freud begins to reconceptualize the pleasure principle and the reality principle in "The Economic Problem of Masochism" (XIX:160 ff.), but it is only a beginning. He distinguishes the so-called Nirvana principle, the tendency to seek discharge, from the pleasure principle. Hitherto he had identified the two. (See *Beyond the Pleasure Principle*, XVIII:55–63, 38–39.) The pleasure principle now is, as it were, the Nirvana principle after Eros has gotten through with it. It now represents the demands of life and libido. The reality principle is now conceived as no more than a modification of the pleasure principle under the influence of the external world. What had been a fundamental opposition in forms of mental functioning is now a matter of fine tuning. (Cp. "Formulations on the Two Principles of Mental Functioning," XII:218–26.)

Love, he speculates, is a force that permeates animate nature. So it is a mistake to think of love just in terms of the libido within a given individual. Love runs through the world that he is investing with his love. So the world he loves must be a loving world. And this suggests that what it is for the world to be lovable is for it to be loving. If we initially restrict our focus to the emerging world of the infant, this seems to be borne out.[69] The infant is, ideally, born into a world of loving parents. And what it is to be a "good enough" parent is, in part, to be in tune with the child's emerging needs, to respond to them in loving and comforting ways, and in this way to reflect, at a higher level of organization, the child's emerging mentality. Without this loving responsiveness and reflection, children tend to die.[70] So it seems that a child needs to be born into a psychological world, a world permeated by mind and the emotions, not only to develop a mind but simply to survive as a functioning organism. As the infant grows into a child, an adolescent and an adult, his world will, in healthy circumstances, tend to expand and deepen. But it would seem that for this expansion to take place, the world itself must maintain a certain responsiveness to and reflection of the emerging person. It must respond to his emerging curiosity and interests and, in so responding, reflect them. We seem then to need the concept of a *good-enough world.*

For the I, Freud says, "living means the same as being

---

69. This is a recurrent theme of Winnicott. See, e.g., the various papers on development in *The Maturational Process and the Facilitating Environment*; as well as *The Child, the Family and the Outside World*. This also seems to be borne out in our interpretation of Freud's analysis of little Hans and of his early treatments of hysterics. In each case, as we have seen, he provided his patients with reassurance and responsiveness to their conflicts.

70. See Spitz, "Genesis of Psychiatric Conditions in Early Childhood (Hospitalism)," *Psychoanalytic Study of the Child*, 1, pp. 53–74; and "Hospitalism: A Follow-up Study," *Psychoanalytic Study of the Child*, 2, pp. 113–17.

loved."[71] Life is possible because the erotic relation between a person and the world in which he lives runs two ways. We have only the most rudimentary understanding of this erotic relationship. We have the barest idea of a good-enough world, and we don't yet know what happens to a person who lives in one. Love is an inner force for development, but we don't yet know what shape this development takes. It is only when we understand this development that we will understand the role of love within human life.

---

71. *The Ego and the Id*, XIX:58. In this case he was talking about the love of the super-I for the I, but the super-I's love is in fact an internalization of the loving world. I shall discuss this in the next chapter.

6

Where It Was,
There I Shall Become

I

It is hard to take love seriously. Analysts tend to dismiss
love as cosmological speculation for which Freud had a
predilection but which goes beyond the bounds or concerns
of psychoanalysis.[1] It is one thing to see the drives as located
in the human being; it is quite another to see them permeating animate nature. So the thought goes, and it is a
plausible line of reasoning. It is also mistaken. For love is
not *just* speculation on Freud's part, and it has distinctive
psychoanalytic significance. As Freud comes to appreciate
that the individual is a psychological achievement, he becomes increasingly interested in the conditions under which
this achievement occurs. The individual, he realizes, cannot
be understood other than as a *response* to certain forces that
permeate the social world into which he is born. And the
individual is a manifestation and embodiment of *the very*

---

1. That Freud did have such a predilection is beyond doubt. See, e.g., *Civilization and Its Discontents*, XXI:119; "Analysis Terminable and Interminable,"
XXIII:245, 247; and *New Introductory Lectures on Psycho-Analysis*, XXII:107.

same forces to which his existence is a response. The individual, Freud discovers, cannot be understood in isolation.[2] Unless we see love not merely as located in the human being but as permeating the world in which he lives, we cannot understand the psychic structure which constitutes the individual.

Here is what we want to know: what happens to a good-enough human being in a good-enough world? For it is in this situation that we see love most clearly in the human and in the world into which he is born. Freud, of course, began from pathology, from the failure of the world or the human to be good enough. Psychoanalysis, in that sense, is a wisdom won from illness.[3] But if we are to understand love, we must work toward a psychoanalytic understanding of health. To restrict our inquiry to a good-enough, rather than a perfect, world prevents our idealization from going too far. Freud insisted that a developing infant must experience frustration if he is ever to perceive an independently existing world. It is from the disappointment that the breast cannot forever magically meet the infant's wishful lips that the infant begins to differentiate himself from the world. And it is through all the frustrating descendants of this primal frustration that the world comes to have psychological reality for him. A necessary condition of there being a

---

2. The idea that the individual cannot be understood in isolation has had a long and distinguished philosophical career. It is a central theme in the social and political philosophies of Aristotle and Hegel, and it has recently come to dominate certain approaches to the philosophy of language and philosophy of mind: see Wittgenstein, *Philosophical Investigations*; Davidson, *Inquiries into Truth and Interpretation*; Burge, "Individualism and the Mental." Obviously, this idea has also had a distinguished career within object-relations approaches to psychoanalysis. But, for Freud, it is the existence of love which underlies the idea that the individual cannot be understood in isolation. (For a summary of object-relations approaches, see Greenberg and Mitchell, *Object Relations in Psychoanalytic Theory*; see also Mitchell, *Relational Concepts in Psychoanalysis*.)

3. See Mann, "Freud and the Future."

world for this person is that it be a world that is not immediately responsive to his wishes. And so, one might say, it is the essence of the world that it could never be better than good enough.[4]

II

Freud discovered the structure of the psyche through the structure of the emotions. He was trying to understand melancholia, or, as we might call it today, depression, and he noticed a family resemblance to "the emotion of mourning."[5] In both there is "painful dejection, cessation of interest in the outside world, loss of the capacity to love, inhibition of all activity."[6] Mourning is the reaction to the loss of a loved one, but, Freud noted, the melancholic is not conscious of any such loss.[7] Melancholia seems to be an emotional orientation without an obvious rationale. Freud's task was to reveal the hidden rationality. The melancholic, he said, must be right in some way.[8] Freud took his cue from the key difference between mourning and melancholia: "In mourning it is the world that has become poor and empty; in melancholia, it is the I itself."[9] In melancholia there is a "lowering of self-regarding feelings" which is not

4. Here, of course, is the natural place of entry for a psychoanalytic account of aggression. See, e.g., Winnicott, "Aggression in Relation to Emotional Development," in *Through Paediatrics to Psycho-Analysis*; Klein, "A Contribution to the Psychogenesis of Manic-Depressive States," in *Love, Guilt and Reparation*.
5. See, e.g., "Mourning and Melancholia," XIV:242.
6. "Mourning and Melancholia," XIV:244.
7. "Mourning and Melancholia," XIV:245.
8. "Mourning and Melancholia," XIV:246–47.
9. "Mourning and Melancholia," XIV:246 (NB: Here is just one example where Freud's use of the expression "the I" or "the ego" does not refer to a particular intrapsychic agency, but to the melancholic person or his soul.)

to be found in mourning.[10] In effect, Freud discovered that one can be emotionally oriented inward as well as outward. Melancholia is mourning directed inward. But for an emotion to be directed inward, there must be an inner *world* in relation to which the emotion provides an orientation. As Freud put it, the melancholic's disorder gives us insight into the structure of the human I.[11] For melancholia to be possible, he argued, there must be a split within the I in which one part "sets itself over against the other, judges it critically, and, as it were, *takes it as its object.*"[12]

This inner world toward which we are emotionally oriented is, Freud discovered, a re-creation of the outer world. Again, he discovered this through the structure of emotions. If one listened carefully, one would find that the melancholic's self-reproaches fit someone else.[13] Somehow, reproaches that would have accurately been directed against a loved one had been redirected onto the accuser. This was not a mere failure of nerve. In his clinical work Freud repeatedly noticed that melancholics had taken on personality traits, mannerisms, aspects of character of their love objects. So, to take an exaggerated but plausible example, a melancholic might berate himself for his stinginess, but in the course of doing a family history it would emerge that his father had been stingy. The reproaches had become self-reproaches, Freud concluded, because the lover had psychically taken the loved one into himself. The loved one was now part of the melancholic's own I! Freud called this process identification, and he explained it as the outcome of disappointment in love. The melancholic had been in love

---

10. "Mourning and Melancholia," XIV:244.
11. "Mourning and Melancholia," XIV:247.
12. "Mourning and Melancholia," XIV:247 (my emphasis).
13. "Mourning and Melancholia," XIV:248.

with someone, but had suffered some blow or loss. Instead of displacing his love onto another person, the melancholic withdrew his love *and his loved one* into himself.

> Thus the shadow of the object fell upon the I, and the latter could henceforth be judged by a special agency, as though it were an object, the forsaken object. In this way an object-loss was transformed into an I-loss, and the conflict between the I and the loved person into a cleavage between the critical activity of the I and the I as altered by identification.[14]

Psychic structure, Freud realizes, is created by a dialectic of love and loss. The structure of the mind is an inner re-creation of the structure of the loved world. Mental structure develops with the infant's increasing appreciation that the loved world exists independently of him and is not immediately responsive to his wishes.

Although Freud discovered identification in his study of pathology, he realized it was the normal process by which an I comes to be. And a moment's reflection on an I's position in the world convinces us that this must be so. For, as we have seen, a necessary condition of there being a world for me is that I love it, or invest it with libidinal energy. Because my love affair is with a distinctly existing world, I must be disappointed by it. A distinctly existing world cannot possibly satisfy all my wishes. Out of the ensuing frustration and disappointment, I am born. Melancholia, or some archaic precursor, must lie at the heart of every I. In fact, Freud characterized identification as a *regression* from object-love to the most primitive form of emotional attach-

---

14. "Mourning and Melancholia," XIV:249.

ment, primary narcissism.[15] "Identification," Freud said, is "the earliest expression of an emotional tie with another person."[16] Identification is thus the most primitive form of psychic response to a loved world. Now, if primary narcissism is, for the infant, an undifferentiated psychic field from which the I and a distinct world of objects emerge, then this original "emotional tie with another person" cannot, for the infant, be an emotional tie with *another person*. The original identification is rather an initial differentiation by which some of the qualities of the loving mother, the loving world, are taken to exist *on this side* of the emerging boundary. This isn't just a mistaken drawing of the boundary by a little cartographer; it is an active taking in. The infant takes in his mother along with his mother's milk.[17] Because the newborn infant is libidinally attached to the world primarily through his mouth, he fantasizes orally incorporating the loved object. Freud is not especially clear, though at times he does suggest, that the loved object is, for the infant, not yet an object. The infant has his mother for dinner, and through that meal both he and his mother come to be.

Identification is, therefore, a psychological act. It is not merely a neurophysiological process by which I passively come to resemble my environment, as though I were a piece of film exposed to the light of the external world. I do not reflect the world, I devour it. The world I take in and re-create on the intrapsychic stage is thus not the world as it is in itself, but the world as it has been psychologically metabolized by me. The mother I eat is the mother that exists for me. But the mother that exists for me, the world

---

15. "Mourning and Melancholia," XIV:249.
16. *Group Psychology and the Analysis of the Ego*, XVIII:105.
17. "Mourning and Melancholia," XIV:249–50. Cp. *Totem and Taboo*, XIII:142; "Instincts and Their Vicissitudes," XIV:138; *Three Essays on the Theory of Sexuality*, VII:198.

that exists for me, is a world I love: and my libidinal investment suffuses the world with my fantasies as well as my perceptions. And thus when I take in the world, and thereby constitute myself, I do not simply mistake myself for the world. I am claiming, in a sense reclaiming, my libidinal investment as mine. I am taking back my own love, transfigured by its interaction with the loving mother. In this sense, the I is an interpretation: I become what I take the world to be.

Of course, in the original identifications, a not-yet-I takes in a not-yet-mother. It is from these identifications that an I begins to form and, as the other aspect of this process, a world of distinct objects comes to be for this emerging I. As psychic structure begins to form, the level and type of identification of which I am capable correspondingly develops. For as there comes to be a world of objects for me, what I can identify with increases in complexity and structure. There is thus established a libidinal dialectic of development. As I develop in complexity, I am increasingly able to appreciate and identify with ever more complex love-objects. And so it goes. Freud recognized that identification could occur at different levels, for he distinguished narcissistic identification, the original emotional tie, from hysterical identification.[18] In narcissistic identification, as we might now put it, an I is being constituted out of a less differentiated field, whereas in hysterical identification an already existing I takes on the more precisely delineated characteristics of a loved object.[19] Narcissistic identification

18. "Mourning and Melancholia," XIV:250. Cp. *Group Psychology and the Analysis of the Ego*, XVIII:105 ff; and *The Interpretation of Dreams*, IV:149–51.

19. See, e.g., Freud, *The Ego and the Id*, XIX:29: "At the very beginning, in the individual's primitive oral phase, object-investment and identification are no doubt indistinguishable from each other."

is the crucial drama of pre-oedipal development; hysterical identification is a hallmark of the oedipal period. This entire dialectic of development is fueled by love and loss. I become an I in response to the fact that there is a separate world that is not identical with me. I identify with the world because I am not identical with it. I take the world in, and thus constitute myself, as compensation.

We seem to have entered a realm in which wishing makes it so. I want to be the father, rather than have him as a sexual object, and, presto chango, I am he! At least, so far as psychic structure is concerned.[20] How could I, the most real of all things, owe my existence to magic? And yet, if I am to recognize primary process as active mind, to acknowledge that I emerge from a less differentiated psychic swirl of drive activity, I must accept that I come to be out of mental activity which, from the perspective of the already developed I, looks like magic. The I, according to Freud, develops out of that reservoir of drive activity he came to call the *it*.[21] The fundamental problem for the I is that it depends for its existence on libidinal energy, but the source of libido is in the drive-driven it. By fashioning itself after a lost love, the I offers itself as dependable compensation for a fickle world:

> When the I assumes the features of the object, it is forcing itself, so to speak, upon the it as a love-object and is trying to make good the it's loss by saying: *"Look, you can love me too—I am so like the object."*[22]

20. See, e.g., *Group Psychology and the Analysis of the Ego*, XVIII:106.
21. *Das Es*, translated into Latin in the Standard Edition English translation as "the id." The expression is introduced by Freud in *The Ego and the Id* (1923).
22. *The Ego and the Id*, XIX:30 (my emphasis). Cp. XIX:58: "To the I . . . living means the same as being loved."

Identification is thus at once the psychological mechanism by which the I comes into being and develops, and it is the means by which the I captures the it's love. Human development is, for Freud, a tale of disappointments. The newborn must learn that the breast is not immediately controlled by his wishes, the five-year-old must renounce his love affairs with his parents, the mourner must accept his loved one is no more. With each disappointment, Freud said, there is an alteration in the I. He described it as the establishment of the lost love-object in the I, and he speculated that it was only by this process of identification that the it could give up its love-objects.[23] Freud thus concluded that "the character of the I is a precipitate of abandoned object-investments and that it contains the history of those object-choices."[24]

Identification can occur at myriad levels of sophistication and development. But at its most archaic level identification is a primary-process mental activity by which the it develops into an I. Since the process is primary, one ought to expect that wishing makes it so. Within the realm of the drives, there is no firm boundary between wishing and reality: that is the hard-won and often painful distinction which characterizes the secondary-process thinking of the emerged I. One might think of identification as the process by which the realm of magic is circumscribed. At the beginning of life there are no firm boundaries between self and world, nor are there firm boundaries between wishing and reality.

---

23. *The Ego and the Id*, XIX:29.
24. *The Ego and the Id*, XIX:29. Cp. *Group Psychology and the Analysis of the Ego*, XVIII:114. "The world," Wittgenstein once wrote, "is *my* world: this is manifest in the fact that the limits of language (of that language which alone I understand) mean the limits of *my* world." The psychoanalytic response now seems to be: 'The I is the world's I: this is manifest in the fact that the I is a precipitate of abandoned object-investments and that it contains the history of those object-choices." (Cp. *Tractatus Logico-Philosophicus*, 5.62.)

The newborn's wishes suffuse his "world." Each recognition of the mother's separateness is by its nature also a frustration and disappointment. In response the mother is taken in, but so are the child's wishes! For where they once held sway over the world, they are now ever more confined to the interior of the child's developing soul. The process by which an I emerges and distinguishes itself from the world in which it lives has a flip side. To recognize the world as distinct is just what it is to keep one's wishes to oneself. Freud emphasized that the I develops out of and is dependent on the seething it because he wanted to lay stress on drives at the core of human life. From the perspective of the development of the I, however, it looks as though the it, by taking its place within a person's soul, has been confined to a reservation.

The identificatory processes by which the it's loves are abandoned and re-created in the developing I involve a "desexualization."[25] It is not just that the love-object has been given up; libidinal energy has been transformed into psychic structure.[26] Love's compensation to humans for living in a world of distinct love-objects is to fuel the process by which they develop into individual I's. One might thus think of psychic structure as *structured love*.

It is a striking fact that the outcome of my love affair with the world is a development in psychic structure. We can imagine a world, almost like ours, in which beings sent out love and took it back in, just as we do, but in which the identifications yielded no development. For identification to be a developmental process, I must be able to appreciate a complexity and structure in the world I love that

25. See, e.g., *The Ego and the Id*, XIX:30.
26. See also *The Ego and the Id*, XIX:55: The I "withdraws libido from the it and transforms the object-investments of the it into I-structures."

outstrips my own. Our libidinal investments, one might say, are good investments: we seem to be able to take back in more than we originally gave out. What I love and what I take back in exists *for me* at a higher level of complexity than I do. Even at the level of undifferentiated drive activity, love must appreciate greater structure; otherwise no I would ever differentiate itself from the world.

The world, for its part, must provide an occasion for that interaction. In a good-enough world, the infant is born into a loving environment, responsive to its needs. Proceeding from the direction of the infant, one might say that love is directed onto love itself, albeit at a higher level of organization and development.[27] And the infant's earliest identifications constitute a taking in of this more organized love. That is how love organizes itself within the emerging individual. Of course, in the earliest identifications there is no firm boundary between fantasy and reality, and thus there can be no firm boundary between what I am and what I would love to be. Freud placed the origin of the ideal-I in these first identifications.[28] The *ideal-I* is the intrapsychic manifestation of what I would love to be, and Freud says it originates in the most primitive and immediate identifications. Freud thus seems to be saying that the ideal-I is on

---

27. Conversely, proceeding from the direction of the parents, one might say that love is directed onto itself at a lower level of organization. But this is part of the process by which the lower-level organization develops.

28. *The Ego and the Id*, XIX:31, 48. Cp. *Group Psychology and the Analysis of the Ego*, XVIII:105. Now, Freud never clearly distinguished the ideal-I from the *super-I*, the agency of conscience, self-observation and self-criticism. See, e.g., "On Narcissism: An Introduction," XIV:93–96; *Group Psychology and the Analysis of the Ego*, XVIII:116, 129. By the time Freud wrote *The Ego and the Id*, he seems to have absorbed the ideal-I as one function of the super-I (e.g., XIX:34). And see *New Introductory Lectures on Psycho-Analysis*, XXII:66. Cp. Wollheim's discussion of the distinction in *The Thread of Life*, pp. 219–21; and Chasseguet-Smirgel, *The Ego Ideal*.

the scene before I am!²⁹ This isn't a confusion. Freud is straining to make a deep point which might be put as follows. Because in the earliest identifications there can be no firm boundary between what I am and what I would be, there can be no firm distinction between I and ideal-I. One might say that both the I and the ideal-I differentiate themselves out of a prior, less differentiated I-state which might be called the *idealized proto-I.* That I emerge from an idealized state is a necessary consequence of the fact that I am formed via a series of identifications with parents who are more organized than I am. But for an I to emerge, the I must be able to distinguish fantasy from reality. This requires not only that the I differentiate itself from the world in which it lives; the I must also differentiate itself from what it would be. An I must be able to perceive itself as part of the world, and to be able to do this, the I must split itself off from the fantasied I-representations. Thus the emergence of an I and the emergence of an ideal-I are two aspects of a single process. What it is for an I to come into existence is to be split from its own sense of what it might be. The sense of distance, of falling short of what I might be, is thus not an accident: it lies at the heart of the I's existence.

In a pathological case the sense of distance will be overwhelming. In one type of pathology, there will be powerful incompatible identifications, so that becoming any one thing entails failing in something else, violating a fundamental prohibition, abandoning part of oneself.³⁰ In another, the infant takes in an unresponsive world and thus develops a

---

29. Thus at times Freud *seems* to be saying that the super-I is on the scene before there is an I to criticize! See, e.g., *The Ego and the Id*, XIX:48.

30. *The Ego and the Id*, XIX:30–31. Cp. Chasseguet-Smirgel, *The Ego Ideal.*

distorted sense of who he is and who he might be.[31] But in a good-enough world, the gap between I and ideal-I will not be too great. Nor will there be fundamentally irreconcilable disharmonies. For the I and ideal-I will be built up by a series of identifications with loved ones who themselves have relatively harmonious souls and who are lovingly responsive to the needs, concerns and abilities of the emerging person. It should be possible for there to be a productive and harmonious tension between the emerging person's sense of who he is and of who he would love to be. *Where ideal-I was, there I shall become.*

III

The ideal-I is not the I's only frontier. Freud famously defined the task of psychoanalytic therapy in these terms: "Where it was, there I shall become." Now, if one translates Freud's *Wo Es war, soll Ich werden* as "Where id was, there ego shall be," there is a danger one will interpret him as saying that the point of psychoanalysis is to replace one psychic agency by another.[32] Freud's concern is not with the replacement of psychic agencies, but with a transformation of the relation in which I stand to my own instinctual life. Freud does of course use *das Ich*—"the I" or "the ego"— to designate a psychic agency, but that is not his only use

31. See, e.g., Miller, *The Drama of the Gifted Child*; Winnicott, "Ego Distortion in Terms of True and False Self," in *The Maturational Processes and the Facilitating Environment*; Kohut, *The Analysis of the Self*.

32. Cp. *New Introductory Lectures on Psycho-Analysis*, XXII:80. And see *The Ego and the Id*, XIX:56. This line is discussed by Bettelheim in *Freud and Man's Soul*, pp. 61–64, and by Loewald in *Psychoanalysis and the History of the Individual*, pp. 11, 18–19.

of the expression. He also uses that expression to refer to what other writers call "the self," "the person," "the individual." The expression "the I" highlights the fact that the self, person or individual is a subject with a first-personal point of view. Freud's ambiguous use is thoroughly productive.[33] For if I may come to be where once it was, then we are at once talking about a transformation of the relation in which I stand to my instinctual life and a transformation in intrapsychic relations. There would be no point in talking about intrapsychic structure if this were not so.

In its most general terms, Freud is talking about the process by which an I differentiates itself from the swirling mass of nature and comes to be. Freud, as we have seen, suggests that the I comes to be by sculpturing itself to the contours of the loved world, thus offering the drives a new love: "Look, you can love me too!" But if we consider what it is about the world that the drives love, it would seem to be the parents' organized, loving responsiveness to the child's needs. A successful identification in a good-enough world ought thus to be more than just the taking in of a love-object. The emerging I ought to embody a loving, responsive relation to (the) it's drives.[34] For that is what it would be to identify with the love-object. That is how love tends toward higher unities in human life. Disorganized love, one might say, is doing more than seeking satisfaction or tending toward discharge. It is attracted to the organized love which responds to its needs, it takes in that love by the fantasied act of identification, and so becomes more

---

33. Cp. Hartmann, "Comments on the Psychoanalytic Theory of the Ego," in *Essays on Ego Psychology*; Kohut, *The Analysis of the Self*.

34. Freud says that the I behaves toward the it "like the physician in analytic treatment." *The Ego and the Id*, XIX:56.

organized. It is in this sense that the world is an occasion for the satisfaction and development of the drives, not just a recipient of discharges.[35]

So the process of psychic organization, in a good-enough development, is not one that leaves disorganized love totally behind. The I should enter into a relationship with the drives which is a re-creation in the internal psychic stage of the parents' loving responsiveness toward the child. The drives are not abolished; they are taken up into a relationship with the I: it is thus that psychic organization is achieved. Psychoanalysts sometimes say that in this process a person *accepts responsibility* for his drives and instinctual wishes. But it often remains mysterious just what is meant and, as a result, it remains equally mysterious why one should accept responsibility. Here it might be useful to ask why Oedipus accepts responsibility for his acts. After all, his fate was determined by the gods even before he came into existence. Why should he accept responsibility for his fate? On a popular understanding of psychoanalysis, we can ask the same question about ourselves. On this understanding, my psychological fate is determined for me, long before I can actively participate in its formation. Why should I accept responsibility for my fate? This is *the other Oedipus complex*. Now, Oedipus, in accepting responsibility for his acts, is claiming that the truth that ultimately matters is, as he says of his blinding, that "I have done it with my own hand."[36] Whatever the gods ordained, Oedipus says, the fact is *that*

35. See "The Economic Problem of Masochism," XIX:160; *The Ego and the Id*, XIX:44.

36. *Oedipus Tyrannus*, 1331; cp. 266. This passage and the issues of responsibility raised by it are discussed with illumination by Williams in *Shame and Necessity*, Chapter 3, "Recognizing Responsibility." As Williams points out, later at Colonus, Oedipus comes to think that he had not been as active as he had previously thought: "I suffered those deeds more than I acted them." *Oedipus at Colonus*, 266–67.

I did it. Oedipus is in effect claiming a part of nature for himself. He treats himself as a locus of activity and in that way demands to be distinguished from the rest of nature. "I am active," Oedipus is saying, "and by my activity I separate myself from the swirl of nature. I am not just a passive sufferer of divine or cosmic forces, I am not just sunk in nature, I act." Now, Oedipus may also *hold himself responsible*: for he may take up an observational stance with respect to himself and judge his acts to be praiseworthy or blameworthy. In holding himself responsible, Oedipus is claiming to be a fit subject for ethical or aesthetic evaluation. Holding oneself responsible is essentially a super-I activity; accepting responsibility is not. In accepting responsibility, Oedipus is making an altogether more elemental claim: "these acts are *my acts*." Oedipus thus constitutes himself as an agent, a locus of activity. *"Where it was, there I am."*[37]

It is this claim which reverberates at the deepest levels of our souls. Long before the traditional Oedipus complex can take shape, each of us is busy devouring nature, actively taking in the world and constituting ourselves as centers of activity. In becoming an individual, each of us is a latter-day Prometheus, wresting activity away from the gods. And because archaic mental life is not abolished in this process,

---

37. While Western literature is full of figures who are (perhaps vainly) striving to avoid (Oedipus) or fulfill (Macbeth) oracles, there isn't a figure who in effect says, "Let's just sit back and watch how this whole thing unfolds." Oedipus does not consult an oracle to find out, passively, what is going to happen to him; he consults the oracle in order to determine what to do.

One might at first hope that there is a simple relation between accepting responsibility and holding (oneself or others) responsible. There is not: the relations between these two concepts are complex and deserve a work of their own. For the moment, I confine myself to the remark that one problem with many self-help books is that they conflate these two concepts. Thus, for example, they effortlessly slide from the claim that if I have cancer I ought to accept that I have it (and try to determine how I shall thus live) to the claim that the cancer is somehow my fault.

but is taken up and incorporated, it is likely that the process itself has archaic meaning for the developing individual. If I am to integrate the it into my life, I must actively take it into my soul. But at the level of archaic fantasies, there is no firm boundary between wish and satisfaction. "Fantasy" is a term we use in higher-level conceptualization to describe mental activity that itself does not distinguish between fantasy and reality. Every fantasy is, at the level of fantasy, also an act. So as wishes become incorporated into the I there must at the level of primary process be an acknowledgment *that I did it*. That is the psychic significance of identifying with one's drives and fantasies. In the gap between the laden phrase "accepting responsibility" and a more neutral "taking charge" lies the difference between a dynamic psychoanalytic understanding of individuation and a self-help book.

Here we can see love at work. Love is not merely an impersonal tendency for unification. Love is *active*: it is working actively in and through mind. And thus it is misleading to think that love *causes* me to develop in complexity and structure, as though love were a distinctly existing cause and I was the effect. The causal, psychological process by which I, for example, incorporate my instinctual wishes and drives *is* love in action. Accepting responsibility is active love. Freud once wrote, rather cryptically, that one must accept responsibility for the evil impulses in one's dreams. "What else is one to do with them?"[38] At first glance, this remark is disappointing. "I did not choose to have these

---

38. "Some Additional Notes on Dream-Interpretation as a Whole," XIX:133. The Standard Edition uses "hold oneself responsible," but it is clear from the context that in terms of the distinction I have made between holding oneself responsible and accepting responsibility, Freud is primarily concerned with accepting responsibility. For he continues: "Unless the content of the dream (rightly understood) is inspired by alien spirits, it is part of my own being." This passage is discussed by Loewald in *Psychoanalysis and the History of the Individual*, pp. 7 ff.

impulses," one might say, "they are not under my control. Why am I responsible for them?" This response looks plausible just so long as one takes the issue to be purely theoretical. That is, one is inquiring whether or not a certain fact obtains—namely, whether I am responsible for my dreams—a fact which either obtains or fails to obtain independently of the inquiry. On this construal, one is taking an objective stance with respect to oneself and one's dreams and asking whether they happen to be linked by the concept of responsibility. Freud's remark is not theoretical in this sense. It is practical: given that these impulses are arising in my dreams, what else am I *to do* with them? The issue is one of activity, of actively determining the shape of the soul. And Freud's answer, contained in the rhetorical nature of his question, is that there is no healthy alternative.[39]

Of course, disowning responsibility is a live option. Repression is the archaic activity by which I deny that certain drives are part of me. Repression is not just making a mistake about where the drives are in fact located; it is an active self-alienation of the drives. Through repression I can hold the drives at a distance, but if I hold them at too great a distance, I become their victim. Freud said that an "unconscious sense of guilt" is present in all severe neurosis.[40] He noticed that patients would often react to progress in the treatment, or some hopeful comment by the analyst, by getting worse rather than better. And he came to think that one of the great blocks to therapeutic success was a patient's stubborn reluctance to give up suffering. There seemed to be a need for punishment which was unconscious: the pa-

---

39. I shall discuss problems with the so-called theoretical perspective in the next chapter.

40. *The Ego and the Id*, XIX:50–55. See also XIX:34, 37; *Group Psychology and the Analysis of the Ego*, XVIII:109–10; *Inhibitions, Symptoms and Anxiety*, XX:117.

tient "does not feel guilty, he feels ill."[41] But, Freud argued, he is guilty and that's why he feels ill. Freud is here treating guilt as a structured orientation, even though he does not have a theory of the emotions which will help him make sense of what he is doing.[42] A conscious sense of guilt, Freud reasoned, is due to a tension between the ideal-I and the I—or, equivalently, to a tension between my sense of who I am and of who I would be. With unconscious guilt, therefore, the ideal-I or super-I must be split off from the I, set over and against it, *holding* the I responsible for the unconscious drives. And the I, for its part, denies responsibility by repressing the drives. This denial the super-I blithely ignores. We have thus a war of separation within the soul. The I sets itself apart from the drives, treating them as alien, and the super-I sets itself apart from the I, judging it critically. This configuration, Freud thought, is common to hysteria and obsessional neurosis.[43]

It seems, then, that the cost of failing to *accept* responsibility for my drives, and thus incorporate them into the I, is that I become liable to *hold* myself responsible for them in a pathological way. Of course, some assessments of my wishes and desires may be part of healthy character development. Holding oneself responsible is not in itself pathological. However, failing to accept responsibility for my drives makes me vulnerable to pathology. In fact, hysteria and obsessional neurosis can be seen as pathologies that arise from failure to accept responsibility; and these pathologies provide the strongest reason within Freudian psychoanalysis for the misconception that the soul has discrete

---

41. *The Ego and the Id*, XIX:50.
42. Cp. *Inhibitions, Symptoms and Anxiety*, XX:169, where as late as 1926 Freud continues to express ignorance of "the psychology of the emotional processes."
43. *The Ego and the Id*, XIX:51–52.

parts. This is the picture of the I as a poor "frontier creature," perched precariously between the demands of the it
and of the super-I.[44] But before concluding that the soul
does have parts, one ought to consider that this configuration is a manifestation of illness. When we inquire into
the transition from sickness to health, the "parts" of the soul
begin to lose their "partness." There is a transformation
from the third-personal stance of holding oneself responsible
for one's drives to the first-personal stance of accepting responsibility for them. The super-I is no longer set over
against the I, but has taken up a more benign residence
within the I, an intrapsychic embodiment of value. Freud
captured both sides well when he called the ideal-I "a *differentiating* grade *in* the I."[45] One might say that the super-
I has been domesticated into an ideal-I. Correspondingly,
the drives are no longer held at such a distance but are
accepted as part of the self. Both these transformations are
of a piece. It is because of a harsh super-I that the drives
are so violently repressed. With the integration of the super-
I into the I, there is new room to incorporate the it as well.
So, rather than being a poor "frontier creature," in health
the I is able to shift the frontiers and encompass the soul.
Thus the usefulness of the ambiguity by which "the I" can
refer either to a psychic agency or to the individual as a
whole.

Hysteria and obsessional neurosis are, from this perspective, pathologies of individuation. The boundaries of the I
have been drawn so as to alienate the drives. The cost is
that they become aliens pounding at the gates. We can now

---

44. See e.g., *The Ego and the Id*, XIX:53.
45. *Group Psychology and the Analysis of the Ego*, XVIII:129 (my emphasis).
Of course, this transformation may set the stage for the development of a healthier
form of holding oneself responsible.

see more clearly how fundamentally the activity of accepting responsibility differs from holding myself responsible. For it is not that in accepting responsibility I offer a different, more benign judgment of these aliens: rather, I open the gates. By that act, the drives lose their alien status. Of course, accepting responsibility may occur at myriad levels of psychological development. But the process to which Freud alludes with his famous dictum, "Where it was, there I shall become," is not essentially occurring at the level of judgment.[46] Accepting responsibility for my drives is not so much a judgment that my instinctual life is part of me— as though that had been true all along and I have just come to realize it—it is the activity by which my instinctual life becomes part of me. Accepting responsibility for the it is, therefore, occurring to a significant extent at an archaic level of mental functioning. Shifting the frontiers of the self is largely an archaic activity.

In a good-enough world, the drives are naturalized citizens. For the I is built up from the infant's earliest identifications with his parents. These parents are responsive to the child's instinctual needs, and this loving responsiveness to the drives themselves ought to lie at the core of the I. For it is this loving responsiveness which the it loves. If, as Freud says, the I forms by attracting the it's love—"Look, you can love me too!"—then the I ought to be a structured acknowledgment of the drives. From this perspective, it is the it that is saying to the I, "Look, you can love me too!" Every I is thus faced with Oedipus' task: to reclaim a part of nature for himself. And it is the essence of Freud's struc-

---

46. That is why a hysteric may judge that he accepts responsibility for his drives and only be elaborating the drama by which he denies it. I began to discuss the distinction between accepting responsibility and holding responsible in Chapter 2.

tural theory of the soul that this is a task of love. It is through love that the boundaries of the soul are redrawn so that what were once taken to be forces of nature I now recognize as my own active mind.

IV

For Freud, love is manifested in human life in the process of individuation. It is in response to a loving world that a human is able to distinguish himself from it. By internalizing that love, the human establishes himself as an individual I, a locus of activity and subjectivity distinct from the rest of nature. The process by which the human soul comes to be is a lifetime activity. Love, Freud said, tends toward ever higher unities, and if we look to the human soul we can see why this should be so. Love, as we have seen, fuels a dialectic of development. Psychic structure can continue to develop because the world outstrips my ability to appreciate it. As I develop in complexity, so does the world as it exists for me. The internalization of structure can thus continue at ever higher levels of complexity and refinement.

Individuation is by its nature paradoxical. I come to be by differentiating myself from the world into which I was born, but success at that project requires that I become a differentiated unity. Because I come to be via fantasied acts of identification, a by-product of that process will necessarily be an ideal-I, a differentiating grade within the I. And although individuation consists in a separation of myself from the rest of nature, the outcome will be healthy only if I include part of nature as part of myself. *Where I am, there it shall be.*[47] My task, as a would-be individual, is to make the it and my super-I my own. Since the development of psychic structure can continue throughout life, this task of individuation can be reenacted at ever higher levels of complexity. Freud and subsequent psychoanalytic thinkers have focused on the earliest stages of development, in part because that is where analyses have tended to lead, in part because of the enormous influence these early stages have on later development. By contrast, I would like to concentrate on late stages of development, because it is here that psychoanalysis and philosophy meet.

The task of including the it within the self recurs at all levels of development. At the earliest stages, as we have seen, the child incorporates the it by identifying with the loving responsiveness which the parents have displayed toward the child's needs. The I begins as an intrapsychic embodiment of acceptance of one's instinctual life. Instinctual life can thus be integrated into the emerging life of the person. Though Freud sometimes writes as though the it were a cauldron that bubbles away, oblivious to the events in the external world, in fact he discovered that it is remarkably responsive to loving responsiveness.[48] The I is differentiated from the it in response to a loving responsiveness found in the world and becomes an intrapsychic re-creation of that loving responsiveness. That is how the I attracts the it's love.[49] And Freud speculated that this

---

47. Cp. Loewald: "where ego is, there id shall come into being again to renew the life of the ego and of reason." *Psychoanalysis and the History of the Individual*, p. 16.

48. See, e.g., *New Introductory Lectures on Psycho-Analysis*, XXII:73–75. And, Freud said, there is no sharp distinction between the I and the it: *The Ego and the Id*, XIX:24, 38. And see *Civilization and Its Discontents*, XXI:66.

49. Freud once said that the it "has no means of showing the I either love or hate," but that cannot be right. If the it could not show the I love, the I would not exist. See *The Ego and the Id*, XIX:59.

might be "the universal road to sublimation."[50] Sublimation, for Freud, is the process by which the energy of the drives is taken up and directed toward "higher," more creative aims.[51] Our greatest cultural achievements, Freud speculated, may be due to sublimation. But in the case of the development of the I, sublimation is an activity that attracts the it's love by responding to it and taking it up to a new level of organization.[52]

Sublimation, then, is a paradigm activity of individuation. For it is an activity that tends toward form while including instinctual life within it. All sublimation, one might say, is an acceptance of responsibility for one's it. Sublimation can occur at all levels of development, but I would like to concentrate on a late stage where actively thinking about accepting responsibility, an activity characteristic of philosophy, can itself be a manifestation of accepting responsibility. For this thinking to be sublimation in the fullest sense, it cannot be merely thinking: the thinking must itself take up and be infused by the instinctual life for which it is assuming responsibility. Otherwise there is the possibility of the empty hysterical gesture: "I accept responsibility!" The thinking must be not so much a recording of an antecedently existing fact as it is the very activity of accepting responsibility. How is this possible? One example occurs within the context of a psychoanalytic therapy. For analysis is a symphony of regression and reorganization: in regression, the analysand strongly experiences his instinctual life; in reorganization he acquires the concepts with which that life can be understood. The analytic interpretation which offers the concepts is, in its way,

---

50. *The Ego and the Id*, XIX:30.
51. See, e.g., *Five Lectures on Psycho-Analysis*, XI:53–54.
52. Cp. Loewald, *Sublimation*.

a loving response to the experienced instinctual life, and the it's response to that responsiveness is to infuse those concepts with life and vigor. In the melody of regression, interpretation and reorganization there is a re-creation in miniature of the drama from which the I emerged.

That is why the recognition that mind is active in the body—that no "mysterious leap" is necessary—cannot just be a *discovery* of psychoanalysis. Properly understood, this recognition is not the discovery of a truth that has existed all along, but a transformation of the relation in which I stand to my instinctual life. It is essential for me to come to see my mind as active in my body for me to be able to accept responsibility for this somatic "thinking." And it is essential to the transformation inherent in accepting responsibility that this recognition not be from the perspective of nineteenth-century science. For to adopt that perspective, I must, as it were, step outside my drives and consider them as mere objects in nature. This is the perspective from which the paradox of the other Oedipus complex arises. For from this perspective it looks as though the drives are determined *for* me rather than *by* me. Why should I accept responsibility for forces that are determining my fate? This puzzle depends on a particular conception of objectivity. The idea is that in order to have an objective view on a subject matter one must be outside of, detached from and non-intrusive with respect to that subject matter. It is from this supposedly external view that my drives take on the appearance of natural objects shaped by natural forces. What seems to get left out of this perspective is my activity. There does not seem to be room to view these forces as manifestations of my active mind.

Philosophers have dealt with this puzzle by offering another perspective. From the "internal" perspective from which I live my life, I am active. It is only when I take up the "external" perspective of natural science that my drives appear to be brute natural forces determining my fate. To avoid the puzzle of the other Oedipus complex, it is urged, one must remain within the internal perspective. For it is only within the internal perspective of my agency that accepting responsibility makes any sense.

This solution is thin and unsatisfying. As soon as one divides up perspectives into internal and external *and places natural science in the external*, one has presupposed that the external perspective gives us the way things *really* are. And insofar as philosophy equates the objective with the external perspective, it exerts an inhibiting influence on the process of accepting responsibility—albeit, at a fairly abstract level. For it is small comfort to be told that around issues of responsibility we should stay within the internal perspective. All the exhortation to stay within the internal perspective cannot finally quell the skeptical doubt that, *really*, there is no reason to accept responsibility.

The significance of Freud's putting love in the world is to challenge the distinction between internal and external perspectives. There is, for Freud, no external perspective from which love disappears. Love is a basic natural force, and so the perspective of natural science must be a perspective that includes love. And since love is manifest in my own psychological activity, there is no perspective from which one can "look down" on the drives as brute natural forces, determined for me rather than by me. One cannot, then, stand outside love and see what it really is. The only objective perspective of love, Freud seems to suggest, is one that works its way through love. Psychoanalysis, which aims at an objective study of man, must itself be a manifestation of man's erotic attachment to the world. And the only objective view of the drives must be one that is by nature transformative of them. The drives are natural forces, to be sure, but they are also manifestations of love, shaped by the loving responses they encounter. The psychoanalytic study of the drives, whose bedrock lies in analytic treatment, is in its essence a loving response to the drives. The internalization of this response is part of the process by which an analysand accepts responsibility. This is a manifestation of love within human life, and there is no external perspective from which it can be revealed as a mere appearance. In this way, Freud placed a wedge between the idea of an objective study of man and the idea of a detached, external, non-intrusive study. If love is a basic force in nature, then we must abandon the idea that an external study gives us the way man really is.

7

Radical Evaluation

I

"Psychoanalysis" is a word which, even without our trans-
lating it, Socrates would have understood. In fact, Socrates
invented philosophy by devising his own peculiar brand of
psychoanalysis. Through an examination of one's own soul,
Socrates believed, the truth would emerge and it would set
one free. For as long as philosophy has existed, which, after
all, is only twenty-five hundred years, it has been concerned
with the relation between self-reflection and freedom. Yet
it has never been clear what self-reflection is, or what freedom is, or why the former should make any contribution
to the latter. Psychoanalysis represents one of the most determined attempts in the twentieth century to work out the
relation between self-reflection and freedom. Indeed, it is
only because psychoanalysis was founded in the treatment
of illness and philosophy tends to focus on health that they
look like different disciplines. As psychoanalysis and philosophy turn their attention to the growth and development
of the individual, their boundaries should fade.

In charting Freud's account of the development of the I, we have encountered three significant ideas: first, that the individual is a response to and manifestation of a good-enough world; second, that the I develops not by abolishing the drives but by incorporating them; finally, that since the I is a manifestation of love, there is no external perspective from which this achievement can be appreciated. These ideas are as philosophical as they are psychoanalytic.

Freud has often been compared with that other great European thinker of the late nineteenth century, Nietzsche.[1] Both were master diagnosticians of unconscious motivation, but the conception of man's place in the world implicit in Freudian psychoanalysis is just the opposite of the nihilism that flows from Nietzsche's work. For simplicity, let us say that nihilism is the view that things in the world have value solely in virtue of being valued by humans. Nihilism portrays a world in which value is contingent, arbitrary, capricious. Of course, psychoanalysis does pay homage to the variability of objects humans can love. Thus Freud said that the sexual drive and its object are merely soldered together. But psychoanalysis also reveals a deeper sense in which the succession of sexual objects is occurring only at the level of appearances. At the deeper levels of psychic significance, it would seem the bonds between sexual drive and object are all but impossible to undo.

From the perspective of Freudian psychoanalysis, it is not that humans make the world lovable by investing it with their love; it is because the world *is* lovable that humans can develop into creatures capable of loving it. Since the form of the world informs the human mind, there are constraints on what form the world can have if there is to be

---

1. Occasionally by Freud himself: e.g., "An Autobiographical Study," XX:60.

a human mind. If the world is too chaotic, too unresponsive, too unloving, then it is unlovable: not because it is actually unloved by any human valuer, nor because it is psychologically impossible for a human valuer to love it, but because in such a world there could be no human valuer.

Nihilism looks plausible if one begins with the human valuer. It then looks as though things are lovable just because they are loved. And there seem to be no constraints on what they might conceivably love, and so no constraints on what is lovable per se. But if we ask what must be in a human soul in order for it to take on the shape of a distinctively human soul, constraints emerge. For if the human mind is formed, as psychoanalysis teaches, by a taking in of qualities in the world and reestablishing them as intrapsychic structure, there ought to be constraints on how the world can be such that the internalization of *that* results in a human mind. For the infant, as we have seen, a lovable world is a loving, responsive world—a world of loving parents who are in tune with the infant's needs and who can satisfy them in a reassuring and caring way. Now, when the infant responds to this responsive, loving world by investing it with love, is he *responding* to its lovableness or is he *creating* lovability by loving it? It would seem that he is responding to it, for the idea that he is creating lovability suggests that it is in his power to love other sorts of worlds than the one he chooses to love. But if we take seriously the idea that the I is a psychological achievement, a "new psychical action," then we cannot assume that he is there before his response, able to choose whether to love this or that world. The world's being a certain way is a condition of his coming into psychological existence. And it is in the activity of responding to this responsive loving world that he comes to be. From the perspective of psychoanalysis, nihilism has come on the scene too late, after the human subject has developed. And it looks at only one side of a complex interaction between a person and the world. The point of insisting that love is a basic force permeating animate nature is to do justice to the fact that man is not just a donor of love, he is also a recipient. It is in this give-and-take that the human soul comes to be. One of the basic elements of the world, according to Freud, is an emotion. Love runs through human nature, and it is through the transactions of love as incarnated in humans that individual persons come to be.

II

But it is not just nihilism that has come on the scene too late. Modern philosophy in general has a tendency to investigate the structure of the human soul in isolation from any consideration of how that structure came about. The thought is that philosophy is only concerned with what the structure of the soul is: how this structure developed is a topic for psychology. The problem with this reasoning is that if the individual is by nature a response to a good-enough world, we may be unable to determine what the structure of his soul is if we remain ignorant of the conditions in which it came into being.

It is distinctive of human beings that they care about the shape of their souls: they care about what values and characters they have, they care about how they should live. Psychoanalysis shows that our concern with how we should live is itself a product of love and loss. It is experiences of separation from loved and loving figures which spur processes of internalization of these love relations. This helps to constitute a psychic structure sufficiently rich to enable a person to care about himself. The creation of the individual and the caring for the individual are of a piece. For it is only with the internalization of these caring relationships that there emerges a creature sufficiently reflective and self-aware to deserve the title of "individual."

In a good-enough world, the outcome of this process will be a certain harmony in the soul. That the world which is internalized is a loving world will allow, on the one hand, the development of a super-I that is loving and tolerant toward the drives and, on the other, the development of an I that is sufficiently attractive to the it as to allow ever greater levels of sublimation, whether in psychic structure or in creative activity. There will, that is, be a more or less harmonious structure established in the soul. But this harmony is of its essence derivative: it is the outcome and re-creation within the soul of the loving relationships in a good-enough world. In that sense, the harmony is a manifestation of and response to love.

Recently, a number of philosophers have argued that freedom of the will can be understood as a certain harmony in the soul: as a harmony between one's values and one's desires, between one's values, desires and one's deep sense of self, or between one's "higher order" and "lower order" desires.[2] Of course, harmony in the soul will provide free-

---

2. See, e.g., Frankfurt, "Freedom of the Will and the Concept of a Person"; Watson, "Free Agency"; Taylor, "Responsibility for Self." This is a development of a conception of freedom which has its roots in Spinoza, who offered an alternative to the traditional account of free will. Traditionally, a person was thought to have a free will if he could have chosen to act otherwise than the way he in fact did act. There are many problems with this account of free will, but the problem that concerns us is that this account seems to ground my actual freedom in terms of something I might have done but didn't. The attraction of explaining freedom in terms of a certain harmony in the soul is that it grounds my freedom in the actual state of my soul, rather than in my ability to have changed that state.

dom *from inner conflict*, but why assume that in this battle-free zone one has achieved any higher freedom than that? Suppose, for example, one's values or "higher order" desires have been instilled in one in an unreflective, coercive way. Even if one is able to make one's "lower order" desires march in step, there is a sense in which one's whole harmonious will is an expression of enslavement to external coercive forces. One cannot tell what freedom a person enjoys just by considering the structure of his soul in this way. For it is at least conceivable that a person may enjoy relative freedom from major inner conflicts and yet the meaning by which he lives may not be his. That is, he is not free *from his environment*, for he has not engaged in a process of separation and individuation. His will cannot be free because it is not *his* will.

Philosophers have tended to start with the soul and then ask what conditions are necessary within it for a person's will to be free. From a psychoanalytic perspective, this inquiry is doomed from the beginning. Since the human soul is a psychological achievement, a response to and differentiation from the world, the fundamental issue cannot be merely internal harmony, but whether one has made one's soul one's own. That, of course, does not mean one will not be influenced by one's environment. It does mean that a process of differentiation must have occurred so that there is a point in distinguishing the person from the environment. It is one thing for a cultural environment to influence a person; it is another for there to be no firm boundaries between a "person" and his environment. In the latter case, we are talking of a person only as a potentiality, as something that might come into being.

The philosophical literature abounds with stories of happy torturers: a person brought up to smile on the cruelty in his soul.[3] To make the case more difficult, let us assume that he was not brainwashed or otherwise coerced into valuing cruelty. Perhaps he was lovingly educated into cruelty, just as others are lovingly educated into concern for others. By now, he accepts his cruelty. He dishes out pain without remorse. Is his will free? The answer must be that we have no idea. On the basis of what we have been told, we do not know if we are dealing with a differentiated individual or someone who exists in a merged state with his parents. We do not, that is, know whether he has a will. And psychoanalysis gives us reason to doubt that the harmoniously willed torturer is a genuine possibility. Again, if one starts with the individual soul, it seems as though cruelty might harmoniously ripple through it. If, however, the individual human soul is in its essence a response to and re-creation of a loving environment, a good-enough world, then there seem to be constraints on what sorts of harmony could plausibly be established. From all we know of cruelty, it is not lovingly instilled. It is cruelty that breeds cruelty: and thus the possibility of a harmonious cruel soul, relatively free from inner conflict and sufficiently differentiated from the cruel environment, begins to look like science fiction.[4]

---

3. See, e.g., Wolf, "Sanity and the Metaphysics of Responsibility."

4. Thus, for example, JoJo in Wolf's "Sanity and the Metaphysics of Responsibility." Wolf adds sanity as a condition for freedom of the will, which she explicates as a responsiveness to the world. However, she can give no real account of what this responsiveness consists in. (See, e.g., her remarks on the insanity of male chauvinism in the previous generation, pp. 56–57.) And because she ignores the conditions in which the human soul is formed, she is able to make it seem as though a harmonious soul could emerge that was, as it happened, unresponsive to the world. What psychoanalysis teaches is that the very formation of a soul is dependent on a certain type of responsiveness. Sanity is a constitutive condition of a fully formed soul. Clinical experience suggests that the closest example of a happy torturer is a torturer who is happier than he normally is when he is torturing. Such people are not stably happy or well-integrated humans. On the whole, it is a tough life to be a torturer.

III

We have been considering some consequences for philosophy of the idea that the individual is a response to and manifestation of a good-enough world. A second significant psychoanalytic discovery is that the individual develops not by abolishing archaic mind, but by incorporating it into the structure of the individual soul. Philosophers have remained more or less blind to archaic mental life. Consider, for example, this refutation of pre-logical thinking:

> Oversimplifying, no doubt, let us suppose it is claimed that [some] natives accept as true a certain sentence of the form "*p* and not *p*." Or—not to oversimplify too much—that they accept as true a certain heathen sentence of the form "*q* ka bu *q*" the English translation of which has the form "*p* and not *p*." But now just how good a translation is this, and what may the lexicographer's method have been? If any evidence can count against a lexicographer's adoption of "and" and "not" as translations of "ka" and "bu," certainly the natives' acceptance of "*q* ka bu *q*" as true counts overwhelmingly. We are left with the meaninglessness of the doctrine of there being pre-logical peoples; pre-logicality is a trait injected by bad translators.[5]

This argument purports to show that there could not possibly be such a thing as pre-logical thinking. Suppose, though, that "*q* ka bu *q*" was uttered during highly ritualized activities. These seemed to the anthropologist like enact-

---

5. Quine, "Carnap and Logical Truth," in *The Ways of Paradox*, p. 102. Quine admits that this is a "caricature" of a doctrine of Lévy-Bruhl.

ments infused with archaic mental activity. The whole point of this regressed drama may be to reassure the tribe that it can have its cake and eat it too! And, at the level of fantasy, it can. Pre-logicality is not necessarily a trait injected by bad translators: it may be a trait recognized by anthropologists sensitive to the archaic irruptions into daily life. To say a priori that the natives *cannot possibly* be accepting sentences that express contradictions is, in effect, to refuse to recognize archaic mental life for what it is: active mind. Here it is not just that secondary-process mind does not recognize archaic mind: it has ruled out the possibility of there being anything mental other than secondary-process thinking. That is, philosophy has here equated mind with secondary-process mind. From the perspective of psychoanalysis, this is at least as constraining as the previous equation of mind with conscious mind.

Throughout philosophical anthropology there runs the axiom that the possibility of interpreting others—as thinking, saying, doing anything—depends on interpreting them as being, more or less, like us.[6] This "principle of humanity" is a priori and non-optional: without it, an interpretation cannot get off the ground. However, although the principle may be a priori, its content is not. We do not know a priori what it is to be *like us*, and thus we do not know and cannot set limits to the behavior in others that we will come to recognize as intelligible. There has been a tendency in the philosophical study of interpretation to slide from "interpreting others as like us" to "interpreting others as rational." For instance, it has been argued that for interpretation to get started, we must find a way of imposing "our logic"

---

6. For a classic statement of this "principle of humanity" or "principle of charity," see Davidson, "Radical Interpretation," in *Inquiries into Truth and Interpretation*.

onto the natives' utterances. That is why, allegedly, we could never properly translate "ka" and "bu" as "and" and "not." This a priori imposition of "our logic" on the natives is, ultimately, a refusal to recognize archaic mental activity in ourselves. It is to say that the domain of the intelligible is restricted to the secondary-process conception of rationality. Psychoanalysis challenges us to redraw the boundaries of the mental. We can recognize as intelligible actions and utterances which, from a rigidly secondary-process perspective, are irrational. Of course, to be able to recognize these actions as expressions of mind, we must be able to find what, from a more relaxed secondary-process perspective, might be called a proto-rationality in them. There is method in archaic madness. We cannot, however, set limits in advance on the domain of proto-rationality. We discover what proto-rationality is by discovering what we can recognize as intelligible in ourselves and in others. Man, one might want to say, is a proto-rational animal: but before we know what we are capable of recognizing as active mind, we have little idea what this claim amounts to.[7]

And yet, if we cannot recognize our archaic mental life,

---

7. Recent philosophy has suggested that meaning is a human creation: it is out of human practices, customs, rituals and institutions that meaning emerges. (See, e.g., Wittgenstein, *Philosophical Investigations*, I. 198–206.) These practices are, however, taken as basic: "What has to be accepted, the given is—so one could say—forms of life" (ibid., p. 226). Philosophy takes forms of life as given because it has been oblivious to archaic mental activity. Once we take archaic mental life into account, we can see that while human practices may well imbue language with meaning, the human practices are themselves infused with archaic meanings. The rituals from which meaning emerges are themselves endowed with archaic meanings which give those rituals shape. In our primal interactions, before we and the world are distinct precipitates, there come to be archaic meanings in our souls. This is our identificatory response to a good-enough world. These archaic meanings help to shape what we are, and they infuse our practices with archaic content.

we must remain ignorant of who we are. For example, one might think of Kant's critical philosophy as one of the great philosophical attempts to describe who we are. The *Critique of Pure Reason* sets out to delimit the a priori characteristics of our minds. We are, Kant says, *discursive intelligences*: we think by applying concepts to objects that are given to us in sensible experience. Our minds may actively impose form, they may shape our experience, but ultimately there is something that is *given* to us.[8] Our experience is not entirely our creation. He contrasted our minds with an *intuitive intelligence*: "for example, a divine understanding which should not represent to itself given objects, but through whose representation the objects should themselves be given or produced."[9] For a divine mind, there is no fundamental difference between thinking and being. A divine mind is not presented with objects in experience; objects spring into being with the divine activity of thinking. Or rather: for a divine mind, the objects' springing into being *is* the thinking. To appreciate our archaic mental life fully, we must recognize that each of us has such a divine mind within ourselves. From the perspective of archaic mental life, there is no firm distinction between wish and satisfaction, between thinking and reality. That is why a dream can be an attempted satisfaction of a wish. And archaic "thinking" just is the objects of thought springing into being—at least from the perspective of archaic mind. We are not then, and could not be, purely discursive intelligences. By failing to recognize archaic mind, Kant misdescribed the boundaries

8. See, e.g., *Critique of Pure Reason*, B137–139. (We do not experience the given as such, but we can reason back from the nature of our experience and the a priori constraints on it to the conclusion that our experience is not purely the product of our own activity.)

9. *Critique of Pure Reason*, B145.

of who we are.[10] And it is crucial to the process of individuation that I incorporate this other mindedness as part of myself. That is the deeper significance of Freud's injunction, *where it was, there I shall become.*

Philosophy, it seems, draws the bounds of mind too narrowly. But in its confinement of our activity, there is a truth toward which it is gesturing. Consider, for example, this delimitation:

Mind is circumscribed by the law of non-contradiction. There cannot be "another form of mindedness" in which it is true that p and not p.

From the perspective of this delimitation, all possibilities of being minded, in one way or another, are possibilities that are circumscribed by the law of non-contradiction. Being minded in any way at all is, from this perspective, being minded in accordance with the law of non-contradiction.[11] And so, from this perspective, a counter-factual conditional like

---

10. Psychoanalysis also provides a way of fleshing out the philosophical understanding of a subject's relation to objects. Kant argued that for an individual, experiencing subject to exist, he must be located in a world of distinct objects of which he has experience. But Kant's formal philosophy cannot tell us what the process of an I coming into being is like for the individual that is coming to be. So although Kant argues that an I must exist in and experience a world of objects, we have only the most abstract sense of what this experience must be like. For Kant cannot teach what the not-yet-I's experience of not-yet-objects might be like. And so we have little idea with what "experience of a world of objects" is to be contrasted. By coming to understand what it is like to become an individual, we come to understand the content of Kant's claim. (*Critique of Pure Reason*, e.g., B131–40.)

11. This is essentially a position I put forward in "Leaving the World Alone" and "Transcendental Anthropology." The roots of this position lie in Aristotle, *Metaphysics*, IV.

If I were other minded, then *p* and not *p* would be true (for me)

must be nonsense: for there is no coherent possibility of my being "other minded" in this way.

Now, once one has recognized archaic mental life, one might be tempted to think that this conditional does make sense. For, after all, archaic mind is another form of mindedness which is not tightly constrained by the laws of logic. And so, one might think:

If I *were* archaically minded, *p* and not *p* would be true (for me).

In fact, this conditional ought to be rejected too, but for a different reason. From a psychoanalytic perspective, the problem is not with an archaic, pre-logical mental life. The problem is rather with the possibility that I could be fully constituted by that life. To put it paradoxically: if I were archaically minded, I would cease to be an I. For psychoanalysis, the issue is not one of mindedness but of individuation. I am a differentiated unity of archaic and secondary-process mental activity. The archaic continues to live on in me, but as a part of a higher psychic organization. In itself, archaic mind is a remnant of pre-individuated forms of life. So as I become archaically minded, I begin to decompose.

That is one reason why the challenge of the other Oedipus complex—why should I accept responsibility for my instinctual life?—ultimately looks so shrill. Accepting responsibility is constitutive of the process of individuation, the process by which I become an I. So understood, the challenge of the other Oedipus complex degenerates into: "Why

should I become an I?" Or, more properly: "Why should
not-yet-I develop into an I?" In fact, Freud offers an answer
to this question. Love, as incarnate in human life, is a force
that tends toward individuation. Given the background condition of a good-enough world, a well-endowed human will
by his very nature tend to individuate. Psychic health is
achieved not by abolishing the it, but by taking it up into
the differentiated unity of the I. The "should," then, is the
should of psychological well-being: the cost of inhibiting
this developmental thrust is one or another form of neurotic
suffering.

IV

But if individuation consists in the incorporation of instinctual life, I ought to be able to glimpse what it is like to be
archaically minded. Perhaps Freud's best-known discovery
is love's faithfulness to its past loves. A person never will-
ingly abandons an established libidinal position, and there
remains within the human soul a permanent possibility for
regression. The stability of mental structure is, Freud said,
"exposed to constant shocks."[12] Given the trajectory of human development, regression must entail a decomposition
of psychic structure. And since psychic structure is built up
via the internalization and structuralization of love relationships, one would expect decomposition to involve a reex-
ternalization and liquification of this love. In extreme states
of being in love, Freud saw both love and structure pour
out of the hapless lover.[13] There is, he noted, a tendency

---

12. *Group Psychology and the Analysis of the Ego*, XVIII:131.
13. See, e.g., *Group Psychology and the Analysis of the Ego*, XVIII:112–14;
"On Narcissism: An Introduction," XIV:98–99.

for a lover to idealize the object of his love: he or she is seen to embody all sorts of valuable qualities, to be beyond reproach, to be everything the lover was ever looking for.[14] This produces the illusion that it is because of these wonderful characteristics that the lover has fallen in love, whereas, Freud says, the situation is in fact the reverse. Because the person is in love, he projects the characteristics he values onto his love.

We see that the object is being treated in the same way as our own I, so that when we are in love a considerable amount of narcissistic libido overflows on to the object. It is even obvious in many forms of love-choice that the object serves as a substitute for some unattained I-ideal of our own. We love it on account of the perfections which we have striven to reach for our own I, and which we should now like to procure in the roundabout way as a means of satisfying our narcissism.[15]

That it is *narcissistic* libido that overflows onto the object makes the point that in this love relation the boundaries of the I are loosening. The distinction between myself and my love is becoming blurred. In an extreme case,

14. Though this tendency is not universal. One of the difficult legacies of the oedipal period for men was the task of reconciling the affectionate and sexual currents within them. Often these currents remain split apart, and a man finds that he admires, idealizes and feels affection for one type of woman, while being sexually attracted to women he regards as base—e.g., prostitutes. The tendency to idealize can only occur in men who have to some degree united their affections and sexual desires. See "On the Universal Tendency to Debasement in the Sphere of Love"; discussed again in *Group Psychology and the Analysis of the Ego*, XVIII:112. See, e.g., Proust's description of Swann's sexual attractions in *Swann's Way*.

15. *Group Psychology and the Analysis of the Ego*, XVIII:112–13.

... the functions allotted to the ideal-I cease to operate. The criticism exercised by that agency is silent; everything that the object does and asks for is right and blameless. Conscience has no application to anything that is done for the sake of the object; in the blindness of love remorselessness is carried to the pitch of crime. The whole situation can be completely summarized in a formula: *The object has been put in the place of the ideal-I.*[16]

This externalization of one's ideal-I is the essence of de-individuation. The person has abdicated his conscience to the external world and, in the process, ceased to be a fully fledged person. The same phenomenon is found in hypnosis where, in an extreme case, the hypnotist takes on the role of ideal-I and the hypnotized person mechanically obeys the hypnotist's commands.[17] In the hypnotic relation, a person's mind seems to have spread out over two people. What, pre-hypnotically, had been the person's will now seems to be *over there* in the hypnotist.

But Freud's deeper point is that it is only from an external perspective that what we have here are two people. "At the height of being in love," he says, "the boundary between I and object threatens to melt away."[18] For this lover, it is not that he is falling in love with another person; he is falling in love with a world that infuses him. Freud thinks that a variety of experiences—the oceanic feeling of limitlessness, of being at one with nature, the experience of eternity, a lover's conviction that he and his love are one—can be explained as the subjective experience of a regression to an

16. *Group Psychology and the Analysis of the Ego*, XVIII:113.
17. *Group Psychology and the Analysis of the Ego*, XVIII:114–15.
18. *Civilization and Its Discontents*, XXI:66.

infantile state before the I was fully differentiated from the external world.[19] "Originally," Freud says, "the I includes everything, later it separates off an external world from itself."[20] In fact, the I is what emerges from this differentiation. What we have is mind spread out over a relatively undifferentiated field: *that from which* I and world will emerge.

Love's nature is to pull us toward ever more complex unities, but the fact that love is love means that there is an ever-present tendency to regress toward undifferentiated unity. And identification is the mode of regression. This may initially seem strange since it is through identification that the I comes to be and develops. But precisely because the I develops by ever more complex identifications, the I can regress by reverting to an archaic form of identification. The identification is archaic in the sense that instead of taking in some perceived quality of the loved one, the person identifies by suspending the boundary between self and other.[21] He is the other and the other is he. Archaic identification is the route by which the I decomposes.

A prominent example of this erotic formation is what Freud called a mass. A mass is essentially a group of non-individuals, a We composed of proto-I's, held together by archaic identificatory bonds.[22] For a mass to form, individuals must leave their individuality behind. They abandon conscience, leave distinctive personality traits behind and enter an archaic mental field where boundaries blur between the thinkings, feelings, wantings, doings of the members. Indeed, it is only from the outside that we can speak of the

---

19. *Civilization and Its Discontents*, XXI:64–69.
20. *Civilization and Its Discontents*, XXI:68.
21. See, e.g., *Group Psychology and the Analysis of the Ego*, XVIII:106–8.
22. *Group Psychology and the Analysis of the Ego*, XVIII:73–74, 129.

mass as having members: from the inside, it is the essence of membership to have shed those qualities that would characterize one as a distinctive member. The mass seems to operate by a "collective mind." The mass mind tends to function at an archaic level.[23] For example, the members of the mass are typically filled with a sense of the invincible power of the group. This is a sign of the omnipotence of archaic mind, where there are no firm boundaries between wish and reality. The members of the group have each abandoned an individual sense of responsibility, and they are willing to participate without inhibition as a homogeneous and anonymous part of the mass. That the mass operates at an archaic level of mental life helps to explain how a "collective mind" is possible. For at the level of archaic mental activity there are no features deeply differentiating your mental functioning from mine, nor at this level are we able clearly to distinguish boundaries between us. Freud speaks of the way an emotion or a neurotic symptom can spread through a group by "mental infection."[24] Among a group of hysterics, a certain emotion, a gesture or fashion can spread faster than pneumonia. The point is twofold: first, each member of the group would like to be like the person with the emotion and, at the level of archaic mental life, wishing makes it so; secondly, at this level, no one has a firm sense of the boundaries between self and other, so there is no clear sense that the emotion is occurring over there, rather than here. It is in this way that emotions can spread through a group with telepathic speed.

The process of de-individuation by which the mass is formed is one in which the internalized ideal-I is undone.[25]

23. *Group Psychology and the Analysis of the Ego*, XVIII:73–81; cp. 129.
24. *Group Psychology and the Analysis of the Ego*, XVIII:107.
25. *Group Psychology and the Analysis of the Ego*, XVIII:130–31.

Internalized structure decomposes, and the erotic bonds that held the individual mind together are now spread out over the environment. They often invest a charismatic figure, a group leader, who functions as a common ideal-I for the mass.[26] Indeed, the mass may be constituted by its common love of the leader, who functions as a mass hypnotist. The group operates largely at the level of suggestion, with a magical sense that it can accomplish great feats.

Freud draws an important contrast between the structure of the army and the structure of the Catholic Church.[27] In the army, the soldiers take their leader as a common ideal-I and identify with and depend on each other for mutual support. In other words, the army is a typical mass.

It is otherwise in the Catholic Church. Every Christian loves Christ as his ideal and feels himself united with all other Christians by the tie of identification. But the Church requires more of him. He has also to identify himself with Christ and love all other Christians as Christ loved them. At both points, therefore, the Church requires that the position of the libido which is given by mass formation should be supplemented. Identification has to be added where object-choice has taken place, and object-love where there is identification. This addition evidently goes beyond the constitution of the mass. One can be a good Christian and yet be far from the idea of putting oneself in Christ's place and of having like him an all-embracing love for mankind. One need not think oneself capable, weak mortal that one is, of the Saviour's largeness of soul and strength of love. But this further development in

---

26. *Group Psychology and the Analysis of the Ego*, XVIII:129, 134–35.
27. *Group Psychology and the Analysis of the Ego*, XVIII:134–35.

the distribution of libido in the mass is probably the factor upon which Christianity bases its claim to have reached a higher ethical level.[28]

According to Freud, Christ is making a demand on his followers that must by its nature destroy the mass. The mass is constituted by its common love for a leader and by archaic identificatory bonds. The mass depends for its existence on a lack of internalized psychic structure in its members. But Christ is asking his followers not to rest content with placing their ideal-I in him: they must now take him back in, identify with him, make themselves over to be like him. That, from a psychoanalytic perspective, is one meaning of eating his flesh and drinking his blood.[29] According to Freud, Christ incarnates the demands of love in its progressive sense. For to take in his love, identify with it so as to embody it toward one's fellow man, is just what it is to develop an internalized psychic structure. One takes in the ideal-I, makes it part of oneself, and by that process separates from the mass. On this interpretation, Christ is demanding no less of his followers than individuation.

From the perspective of the mass, Christ's demand must be an intolerable insult. For it is not just that this demand happens, as a matter of fact, to entail mass destruction. Individuation must be a crime, for it threatens the mass's

---

28. *Group Psychology and the Analysis of the Ego*, XVIII:134–35.

29. It is a mistake and vulgarization of psychoanalysis to think of this or any other interpretation as providing *the* meaning of an act, image or symbol. One of Freud's most important discoveries is the overdetermination of meaning: a given act or symbol will regularly have myriad, often incompatible meanings. Thus, for example, the fantasy of devouring the mother can simultaneously express both love and hate. And a dream-image may have both oedipal and pre-oedipal content. To search for the meaning of any act is to flatten psychoanalytic theory and to express a thin appreciation for the richness of human symbolizing activity.

intoxicated sense of grandiosity. It is an injury to the infantile narcissism that permeates the mass and it must be met with rage, punishment and revenge. No one likes a party poop. Individuation is at once the great promise of the West and a perpetual threat to the mass bonds that bind us together. Thus a drama in which this promise is made only to be broken is acted and reenacted throughout Western history: in Christ and his crucifixion, to be sure, but also in the emergence of Jewish conscience and the recurrent anti-Semitic backlash, and indeed in the primal crime against philosophy, the execution of Socrates. The great martyrs of Western civilization are martyrs to the cause of individuation.

Freudian psychoanalysis teaches us that this is a drama that is played out within the individual soul. For the individual develops not by abolishing the drives, but by taking them up and incorporating them into the life of the emerging person. But if this primitive mental activity continues within the deeper layers of the individual's soul, then the individual is not only someone who has differentiated from the mass, he is someone who preserves the mass within him. The individual is in the paradoxical position that he must, on the one hand, separate from the mass, but, on the other, retain within his soul the archaic mental life which experiences individuation as an outrage to its omnipotence. Every individual must, at some level of his soul, feel that he has committed a crime.[30] So one meaning of original sin may be that humans are forever tempted by a thrust toward autonomy and separation. Adam ate at the tree of knowledge, but the effect of eating was to take that knowledge

---

30. See Loewald, "The Waning of the Oedipus Complex," in *Papers on Psychoanalysis*.

in: now he could judge right and wrong *for himself.* That is the crime of individuation.[31]

V

In fact, Adam did not take the sin of individuation very far. After all, he got his knowledge *from an apple.* Although he could now judge for himself, his knowledge was given to him by authority, and thus his separation from that authority had to remain partial. Psychoanalysis encourages a more radical separation. Like the incorporation of the it, the process of taking over the super-I and making it one's own is a task that can occur at ever higher levels of development. Herein lies the third psychoanalytic idea whose philosophical consequences I would like to explore: if the I is a manifestation of love, there is no external perspective from which this achievement can be appreciated.

In the early stages of development, a child's ideals and norms do not seem to be located in him at all. They are *over there*, operating in his parents and cultural environment. It is the parents' utterances of values, prohibitions and norms that have efficacy for the child. It is the internalization of those values, their active operation within the individual psyche, that helps to constitute an individual mind. But once values and norms have been firmly internalized, and there now exists within the child a structured super-I, the task of making the super-I one's own can be readdressed at a higher level. It is by now almost an analytic

31. Of course, Christ claims to redeem humanity from the consequences of that first sin. On the interpretation offered here, both sin and redemption consist in the same act: individuation. This may appear contradictory; but this is the type of contradiction which is typical of archaic mental functioning.

commonplace that one of the distinctive tasks of adolescence is to effect a transformation by which one's values and norms are no longer direct internalizations of parental norms, but have been somehow mediated in such a way as to make them distinctive and expressive of the emerging mature adult.[32] But analysts are not very clear on what this process is or on how it is supposed to occur. And no wonder! For this process is one which has troubled philosophers at least since the time of the ancient Greeks—that is, since the time that there was any activity recognizable as philosophy. Socrates, Plato and Aristotle successively made it clear that humans are distinctively able to raise the question of how they wish to live their lives *as a whole*. And unless we can answer this larger question of how our lives are to be lived, we may not be able to answer the most immediate practical question: "what shall I do next?" For I may not have any idea what to do next if I do not understand how that next action fits into a larger life plan. Our immediate practical concerns thus open out onto philosophical reflection, and philosophical reflection in turn opens out onto a *radical* evaluation of our lives, our characters, our values.[33] For we are not now concerned with whether this or that action fits harmoniously with our character or our values: our values and character themselves are up for evaluation.

Psychoanalysis and philosophy meet in the idea of a rad-

32. See, e.g., Blos, "The Genealogy of the Ego Ideal," "The Contribution of Psychoanalysis to the Psychotherapy of Adolescents" and *On Adolescence*; Anna Freud "Adolescence"; Jacobson, *The Self and the Object World*, pp. 170–93; Lampl DeGroot, "On Adolescence"; Ritvo, "Late Adolescence: Developmental and Clinical Considerations." Note that one of Callicles' criticisms of Socrates is that he is carrying a task of adolescence on into old age: "It is fine to have a share in philosophy far enough for education, and it is not shameful for someone to philosophize when he is a boy. But whenever a man who's now older still philosophizes, the thing becomes ridiculous, Socrates." Plato, *Gorgias*, 485a (trans. Irwin).

33. Cp. Taylor, "Responsibility for Self."

ical evaluation. What from a psychoanalytic point of view is a late stage of individuation is, from a philosophical point of view, the distinctive task of human beings. For Socrates, the unexamined life is not worth living.[34] It is not, that is, worth living for a human being: for it is through his examination that a human distinguishes himself from the rest of nature. From the Socratic perspective, the human "distinguishes himself from the rest of nature" in the sense that he carries out a distinctive and special task which is unavailable to the rest of nature. Insofar as he shuns this task, he is living a merely animal existence: this, for Socrates, is not worth living. By this same activity, a human "distinguishes himself from the rest of nature" in the psychoanalytic sense that he continues a process of individuation and differentiation. The parental and cultural norms, once internalized, are now taken up at a new level.

Philosophy and psychoanalysis, each in its own way, encourage the same crime. For Socrates, no values should be accepted simply because they are given by an authority, whether that authority be Athenian society or divine agency. There will always be a further question of whether these values are wise or good, and that question can ultimately be answered only by the individual. Psychoanalysis encourages a person to work through the particular meanings by which he lives his life: nothing is to be taken for granted or accepted merely on authority. In this sense, psychoanalysis commits a crime, and one should expect it to meet with the hostility that a mass displays toward any force for individuation.

However, it is not clear how radical evaluation is even possible. If, on the one hand, it is from within the perspec-

---

34. Plato, *Apology*, 38a.

tive of one's values, it would seem that one has not performed this distinctive human task. One has not *radically* evaluated one's life; one has simply evaluated it from the perspective of certain values. There is the danger that one's self-endorsement (or self-criticism) will be distorted or biased or will beg the question. On the other hand, if one could genuinely step outside one's values, what perspective could this be? On what basis could one make any judgment at all?[35] It seems that we are driven by a need for an Archimedean point, an absolutely objective perspective, but we have no idea what such a perspective might be like, nor do we have any idea how any judgment at all might issue from this perspective.[36] Psychoanalytically speaking, the idea of an external perspective is problematic: do we need a new psychical agency, a super-super-I, to judge the super-I? And if so, what agency is going to evaluate the super-super-I? Clearly, it would be advantageous if we could conceive of radical evaluation as a transformation that goes on within the super-I itself, as a judgment that does not require a mysterious external perspective, and yet it would also be advantageous if we could do justice to the purported experience we have of standing outside our characters, lives and values and judging them as a whole.

If love is, as Freud thought, a basic force, there ought to be no absolutely external vantage point from which a radical evaluation could occur. The process of forming one's values, of testing and evaluating them, of making them one's own, is itself part of the process of individuation. That is, it is an act of love. Thus if radical evaluation is a legitimate and coherent endeavor, there must be a way of understanding

---

35. Cp. Hegel's criticism of Kant in, e.g., *Phenomenology of Spirit*, §§ 599–671; *Philosophy of Right*, §§ 105–40; *History of Philosophy*, III, pp. 457–64.
36. Cf. Clarke, "The Legacy of Skepticism."

it as a manifestation of love, not an evaluation of love from the outside. Of course, it does often *seem* as though in evaluating our lives we are standing outside, looking on. Psychoanalysis is of help in explaining this sense of detachment. For the super-I is not merely the intrapsychic manifestation of values, ideals and prohibitions; it is the internalization of an *observer* of the self. It is one of the ironies and paradoxes of human existence that the self comes into being by the internalization of a self-observer. Now, if the super-I is this intrapsychic observer, we can account for the purported experience of self-observation in the activity of radical evaluation without having to assume that we are in fact taking up a mysterious external perspective. Psychoanalysis explains why we *seem* to be able to take up this perspective, while both psychoanalysis and philosophy make us suspicious that we can do so. Thus it is that a development within one's values and character can be experienced as a stepping outside of them.

But if the sense of an external perspective is an illusion, how can radical evaluation occur? To understand it, one has to see it as a late stage of a process that begins at birth. It is, as we have seen, distinctive of human life that humans care about themselves.[37] They care about the types of lives

---

37. In fact, Frankfurt's structure of second-order and first-order desires is meant to capture the idea that persons distinctively are creatures who care about their wills ("Freedom of the Will and the Concept of a Person"). It does not do so for two reasons. First, it is possible for a person's first-order desires to be in harmony with his second-order desires and yet that person to be relatively indifferent to his will. It may, for instance, be that a person wants to be a heterosexual and that he in fact does desire members of the opposite sex. Yet all of this may not matter to him. The problem with Frankfurt's formulation is that while a second-order desire may reflect, it is itself insufficient to express an emotion as complex as caring. Second, the concern for our wills is reflective, but a second-order desire need not be. A second-order desire is defined solely in terms of its structure: viz., a desire to desire X. So, for example, the desire to be more heterosexual than I am is second-order, but it need not be conscious. Thus a person's reflective concern for his will need not be captured by second-order desires.

they are living. This concern ultimately opens out onto a Socratic reflection on one's life and values, but psychoanalysis discovered that this concern is present in embryonic form at the earliest stages of the development of an individual I. This self-concern begins with an internalization of the loving environment. This begins a process of differentiation from the environment by which an ever more complex human being is able to differentiate himself still more from a loving environment whose complexity he is ever more able to appreciate. In this way, love promotes autonomy. For the successful outcome of this interactive process between external and internalized love is an autonomous individual: one who may care for and depend on his environment, but one who has essentially differentiated himself from it.

If love promotes autonomy, it must also encourage radical evaluation. For the latter stages of becoming autonomous must be subjecting the value of autonomy to scrutiny and making it one's own. It is, in any case, in the nature of autonomy as an ideal that a person should call it into question. One might say that the value of autonomy has not fully developed in a person's soul if he is not yet motivated to question its value. In that sense, autonomy is a *reflexive* value: it ultimately calls itself into question. And what is remarkable about the radical evaluation of autonomy is that it is no threat to the endorsement of autonomy that one recognize that the endorsement is coming from within an outlook that values autonomy. From outside a life that values autonomy, autonomy may well appear threatening, overwhelming, burdensome. It is, after all, autonomy that can make a mass very angry. But the recognition that there is a perspective from which autonomy is not worth it does not undermine the "internal" perspective in which autonomy is its own reward. In that sense, autonomy is *self-validating*: it is the successfully individuated person who can successfully carry out a radical evaluation of autonomy. It would seem to be a token of this world being a good-enough world that this is possible. For if love promotes a process of individuation, a later stage of which is subjecting the value of autonomy to scrutiny, it would be a frustrating world indeed in which autonomy could not pass its own examination. That would be a world in which love promoted a process that could not in principle be completed: a world which encouraged individuation but in which a developed individual would realize, at a late stage of individuation, that he could not endorse or validate his values.

There is a tendency to believe that any "internal" validation must be non-objective: it is the external perspective that gives us the way things really are. This tendency derives in part from a conception of objectivity, worked out in seventeenth-century science, in which the objective view of the world is not from within any particular human perspective, but from no perspective at all.[38] In part, this tendency is a precipitate of about three hundred years of viewing the world as in itself valueless. Value, on this scientific image, is projected onto the world by humans.[39] But if, as Freud thought, love is a basic natural force, this scientific image must be rejected. What is happening in humans is not the projection of value onto inert nature, but the emergence of value in nature. The emergence of autonomous individuals is itself a manifestation of love's developmental thrust, and part of that development is radical evaluation.

---

38. See Williams, *Descartes: The Project of Pure Enquiry*, especially the discussion of the absolute conception of reality, pp. 65–67, 211–12, 245–49, 301–3.
39. See, e.g., Mackie, *Ethics: Inventing Right and Wrong*.

Radical evaluation, then, cannot possibly be going on from the outside: it is itself a manifestation of love. Nor can an external perspective give us the way things really are. The perspective outside love must be one of developmental failure and pathology. If love is a basic force, the only objective validation of autonomy must be an internal validation: one that occurs within an outlook that values autonomy.

VI

Psychoanalysis, by its nature, promotes autonomy. In fact, it is itself a manifestation of the development of autonomy in the world. As such, one should expect the validation of psychoanalysis to emerge from within a perspective that values autonomy. It is by now a commonplace that psychoanalysis does not have moral values of its own: in particular, that it does not try to instill a set of moral values in analysands. This commonplace needs qualification. Of course, psychoanalysis is not in the business of directly instilling any values, nor does it offer any direct answer to the question, say, of whether a person should or should not commit adultery. However, psychoanalysis is by its very nature an activity that encourages the process of individuation in the analysand. It is not legitimately open to an analyst to allow an analysis to continue in which he remains indifferent as to whether what emerges is further individuation or progressive de differentiation and merging. Psychoanalysis by its nature values individuation.

One might be tempted to think that the value of individuation is so abstract that it would allow any particular, concrete values to fall within its compass, but this is not so. Although psychoanalysis might have no *immediate* answer as to whether a person should or should not commit adultery, it would inquire into its meaning for the analysand. If the predominant meaning was that promiscuity allowed for a fantasied merging with oedipal objects, then the analysis would be committed to a process that freed the analysand from these oedipal attachments. Of course, there is truth to the claim that the analysis has freed him to become promiscuous (as well as to cease from being such), but if that is all we say, we ignore the way in which the value of individuation has implications for the continued life of more particular values.

If psychoanalysis values individuation, it must value the values that can be embodied in an individuated life. Although it may not be clear what particular values fall within this range, it would seem that there are constraints on what a truly individuated person can value. For example, although psychoanalysis may acknowledge that moments of merging, and suspension of boundaries, may lend vitality to the human spirit and encourage its further development, it must also recognize that on the whole it is committed to overcoming the values of the mass—the values of omnipotence, de-individuation and lack of responsibility. We have seen that radical evaluation is constitutive of individuation, for it is constitutive of making the super-I one's own. But if radical evaluation requires that values be both reflexive and self-validating, it would seem that there are many values that cannot meet these tests.

For Freud, love is an active force that promotes the development of ever more complex unities. In humans it encourages individuation: a taking up of the drives, on the one hand, a taking over of the super-I on the other. This process is plausibly conceived as a manifestation of love, not only because individuation is an internalization of a loving environment but also because it is only when we manifest this emotional orientation toward our drives and values that individuation can occur. It is only when repression is replaced by an acknowledgment of the drives that they can be taken up and sublimated. It is only by our concern for our lives that we can take up our values and make them our own.

This emotional orientation is re-created in microcosm in the phenomenon of a good-enough interpretation. It is not sufficient for an analytic interpretation to be accurate. An accurate description of unconscious motivation will fail as an interpretation if the material it describes is so far from the analysand's awareness that the concepts, for him, remain empty. It will also fail if it is delivered in such a way—whether in timing, wording or tone—as to provoke the analysand's resistances. A good-enough interpretation must, to its core, manifest a loving acknowledgment of the drives. The drives respond by filling the interpretation with life and meaning for the analysand. The analysand is able to take over the interpretation, and the interpretation itself becomes a sublimated expression of the drives it was trying to understand. It is in this sense that drives are striving toward being understood. Indeed, they are striving toward self-understanding. They respond to loving concern by sublimating into a higher psychic structure: a secondary-process conceptualization that interprets the drives themselves. But a good-enough interpretation is more than a secondary-process conceptualization. It is a conceptualization that is lovingly directed toward and in touch with its "object." A good-enough interpretation is thus structured like an emotion. For the interpretation is itself a sublimation, an organized manifestation of love, and it is lovingly directed toward the drives which are less organized manifestations. And so the acceptance and internalization of a good-enough interpretation is part of an emotional reorientation toward one's inner and outer world.

Here a comparison with Aristotle's conception of form might be of help.[40] For Aristotle, every living organism is a composite of form and matter. Form is an active force in the organism for the development of structure. Form, that is, promotes the development of form in living things. Form thus exists at various levels of organization. In the embryo or youth, form exists as a potentiality or force for development.[41] A mature adult's form, by contrast, is a completed structure. It is an active mode of functioning which preserves that structure. Now, as the living organism acquires structure, it becomes more intelligible. It is in the healthy, functioning adult that the inquiring scientist can discover the principles or organization of that species. Only then can he understand what the youthful striving to acquire form was a striving toward.

It is as though the developing organism is striving to be understood. Aristotle took this possibility seriously. As the scientist studies the principles of organization and functioning of a living organism, these principles impress themselves on the inquiring scientist's mind. His mind comes to reflect the structure he has discovered in the organism. A mind that has understood the form and is actively thinking it has itself taken on the form it is thinking. And as he teaches others about this structure, he is expressing the form

---

40. I discuss this in *Aristotle: The Desire to Understand*.

41. A *dynamis*, often translated as "potentiality," but one should also understand this *dynamis* as an active force or power in the organism.

itself, now at the level of thought. Mind actively contemplating form is the form itself at its highest level of activity. Aristotle called this activity divine. God is actively thinking form and, as such, is form at the highest level of activity. Living creatures, in striving to grow and acquire form, are doing the best job they can to imitate God's activity. In striving to imitate God, they are striving to be understood. Humans distinguish themselves from the rest of nature by the fact that they can participate in the divine activity of understanding.

In a similar way, unconscious motivation can be thought of as striving to be understood. Of course, in the most basic sense, unconscious wishes are striving to get themselves satisfied. But the fact that love is a basic force in the world means that these primitive mental forces also incline toward higher levels of organization. One sees this in the way that the I develops from the it: internal organization is the it's compensation for its frustrating love affair with the world. One sees this also in the way that a good interpretation both relieves the pressure of an instinctual wish and informs its content. The relief indicates that the interpretation provides a certain satisfaction for the wish—as though this is what the wish has been striving for. But the interpretation is an expression of the wish itself at a higher level of organization. In this way, the wish strives to acquire form, a form in which it can be understood. In fact, the activity of understanding the wish—the grasping of a good interpretation— is an expression of the wish itself at its highest level of development. It is also a sublimated satisfaction of the wish. In his study of dreams, Freud discovered that at the most archaic levels of mental functioning, the expression of wish can provide a gratification of sorts. Now again we discover that the most sublimated expressions of the wish can provide sublimated satisfactions.[42]

It is precisely this sublimated satisfaction that provides the validation of a good interpretation. An analysand in a good-enough analysis may even consciously experience this satisfaction. There is the release of the upward pressure toward expression of an instinctual wish. There is the relief in taking another step from passivity to activity: from a position in which one's life is lived by meanings over which one has little understanding or control to a position in which one actively lives according to meanings one has helped to shape. There is pleasure in coming to accept the life one is coming to form. There is satisfaction simply in coming to understand oneself. There has, of course, been a sustained and fine-grained discussion within psychoanalysis of what a good interpretation is, how to formulate it and how to distinguish good from bad interpretations. And psychoanalysis must be one of the last master crafts in the modern West: the ability to listen to the unconscious mental processes in another and give them back to that person in words he can understand and use is an art that can be refined to ever higher levels of sensitivity and sophistication throughout a life. But in the end the validation of a good interpretation must be internal. It is within the context of an analytic therapy that an interpretation can be confirmed or disconfirmed.

It is the necessarily internal nature of validation that has provoked the greatest hostility to psychoanalysis. Some of that hostility is justified. Some analysts have and will con-

---

42. It is important to keep in mind that this satisfaction is highly sublimated; and thus it ought to be distinguished from the plethora of neurotic gratifications that can easily occur in the analytic situation: e.g., the unanalyzed fantasy of the analyst as an ideal loving parent and the analysand as an ideal child.

tinue to use the internal nature of psychoanalytic validation
defensively. It is, as is well known, all too easy to blame a
bad interpretation on a hapless analysand: "the reason the
interpretation has not been accepted is the analysand's resistance to cure, his hostility to the analyst," et cetera, et
cetera. It is a sad truth that not all analysts are good enough,
and the anger provoked by a bad-enough analyst is, I believe, understandable and justifiable. But I am not presently
concerned with this anger so much as with a global hostility
directed toward psychoanalysis. Because psychoanalytic
interpretation can only be validated within the context of a
psychoanalytic therapy, the objection goes, psychoanalysis
cannot be an "objective" science, but must be accepted as
a matter of faith. Indeed, psychoanalysis has sometimes been
compared to a religion: only from within the faith does
psychoanalysis seem persuasive.[43] Of course, there *is* a se-
rious question as to how one tests, adjusts or legitimates
psychoanalytic theory, given that the criteria of evaluation
are, broadly speaking, internal. How does one criticize, alter
or even undermine a theory from the inside? Simply to
dismiss psychoanalysis as a "matter of faith" is to ignore this
question. It is to assume that an objective science must be
evaluable from the outside, from a neutral perspective which
does not assume the concepts or methods of the science.
But *that* is to assume that the concept of a science is in good
shape: that the only issue is whether or not psychoanalysis
lives up to its claim to be one. It is this assumption on which
Freud's idea of a science of subjectivity casts doubt. If one
takes the idea of a such a science to heart, one cannot just
start with the category of science and ask whether psychoanalysis fits into it; the very category of science must be

43. See, e.g., Popper, *The Open Society and Its Enemies*, II, 242–43.

reevaluated. Freud's contribution is not so much to add a new offspring to the existing family of sciences as to encourage us to rethink the basis of kinship.

Freud, as we have seen, did not pursue this line of thought. And neither, for the most part, have subsequent psychoanalytic thinkers. In response to the charge that psychoanalysis is not a science, they have argued that it can, after all, be adapted to the methods and procedures of the empirical sciences; and, more generally, they have tended to adopt the tone, style and vocabulary of papers written in the uncontestably empirical sciences.

Rarely in life is one given the opportunity to become conscious of an assumption by which one's own culture lives. But in this debate—"It is not a science"/"Yes it is"—one can start to see an obsessional strategy being played out at the cultural level. What assumption does this debate hide and protect? That the world is itself devoid of value, purpose or meaning. For if the world were purpose-full, there could be no objection in principle to a science that embodied the very purpose it investigated in nature. It is because the world is assumed to be neutral that science must somehow reflect that neutrality. It is this shared assumption which Freud's postulation of love challenges.

To see this, let us consider a symptom. Within the debate over the validity of psychoanalysis, both sides agree that the ultimate insult is to categorize psychoanalysis as a religion. Certainly, both sides would agree to the following conditional: *if psychoanalysis is a religion, then it is not a science.* And yet, the question of what a religious outlook is—what is the position into which critics want to push it and from which defenders want to protect it?—is one which both sides of the debate ignore. "Religious" is used merely as a pejorative term to mean "not scientific."

Either religion or science: what grounds the assumption that we must choose? One reason is that religion views the world as imbued with value, purpose and meaning; and it is assumed that science cannot possibly see the world that way. It is difficult for us even to imagine the possibility that science and religion might be, not just compatible, but of a piece. We are all familiar with the pablumy apologia for religion—that it can coexist with science—but we have lost a sense of how science might itself be the expression of a religious outlook. Have we repressed it? After all, the idea of a dichotomy between science and religion is relatively recent in the history of human thought. One consequence of placing love in the world is to question that dichotomy.

Let us count the ways of love. Love is active. It flows through humans, but it is larger than human life. It is through love that humans, and the rest of living nature, acquire form. Love tends toward higher organization and form, but humans do not acquire form by passively being affected by love. What it is for love to run through a person is that he himself becomes a locus of activity. That is what it is for love to permeate our nature. A person's activity may be an expression of love, but there is no "outside" perspective from which this activity is revealed as a mere illusion of agency. There is no "neutral" perspective of science from which love disappears. And even the most abstract and theoretical sciences are manifestations of man's erotic attachment to the world.

The very presence of love in the world demands a response from man. In fact, the individual I is, in his essence, a response to love: it is from the internalization of love that an I is constituted. And I develop in structure by repeated internalizations of a good-enough world. For me to develop into a good-enough person, there must be enough goodness running through the world: it is this which I internalize and use to constitute myself. In this sense, too, love is meaningful. In my primal interactions, before I and the world are distinct precipitates, I respond to the world by taking in and shaping myself according to its meanings (as archaically understood by me). And love has a developmental thrust: healthy development is toward individuation and autonomy. One of the manifestations of love is that the good-enough world always outstrips my ability to develop. Thus, however developed I become, I can continue to appreciate new complexities, new meanings in the world. That the good-enough world always outstrips my current ability to appreciate it means that there is no upper bound to human development set by the world. However much I have grown, a good-enough world is calling out to me to respond by growing in depth and structure. One of the deeper meanings of the idea of accepting responsibility is to recognize that I am, by my nature, a response to love. Individuation is my response. It too is a manifestation of love. Love thus tends toward the creating of beings for whom a response— that is, individuation—is a fundamental issue.

Love is mindful. At least, at its higher levels of development love works through and is manifested in mind. Identification, the core activity by which an I comes to be, is a psychological act. This cannot be appreciated from a purportedly "scientific" perspective, a purely third-personal perspective which abstracts from subjective experience. One cannot abstract from a person's subjective experience without making mysterious what it is for him to be. So if love is a genuine force in the world, the so-called scientific perspective must be scientistic. If science is to capture human reality, its bounds and methods must be redrawn. Indeed, science would have to give an internal account of itself: for science is, after all, an act of unification, a development of a higher complexity, an act of love. It is, then, only because love is a basic force in nature that there is a science of subjectivity; and only a science of subjectivity is capable of discovering that love is a basic force in nature.

Should we conclude that Freudian psychoanalysis is, after all, a religion? I do not think so; for I do not believe that the concept of religion is in better shape than the concept of science. It is not that we lack religious conviction, but that we have lost any clear sense of what it is to have it. For example, one need not believe in a creating or personal God to manifest a religious outlook.[44] Nor need one even believe that God is transcendent: it seems one may believe that the divine is immanent in nature. But how could the divine be manifest in nature? What sort of a force should we be looking for? What sort of a divide might there be such that before one crosses it one is just a natural scientist looking at a religiously inert world and after one crosses it one may still be a natural scientist but nature has been transformed? We are not in a position to answer these questions. Freud's legacy is to raise them: once one takes the idea of love seriously, they can no longer be ignored. Of course, Freud himself tried to place psychoanalysis squarely in the sciences; but the ironic upshot of his doing so is that it is no longer clear what the category of science is.

And so the point of these reflections cannot be to decide into which of two pre-existing categories, science or reli-

---

44. Aristotle's God, for example, is neither. Freud, as is well known, thought that religious belief was an illusion: a belief caused by a wish (*The Future of an Illusion*, XXI:30–33). From our current perspective it seems that he did not carry his analysis far enough. For even if belief in a benevolent, omnipotent, personal God is a projection of an infantile image of the father onto the world, might that not be an archaic representation of something Freud himself believed: namely, that love is a force permeating nature?

gion, psychoanalysis fits. Nor can it be to show that it is in fact all right for psychoanalysis to fit into both. For psychoanalysis challenges us to reevaluate the most basic categories of human understanding. Our task, then, is not to locate psychoanalysis in the world, but to work through psychoanalysis to relocate ourselves.

ACKNOWLEDGMENTS

I would like to thank the John Simon Guggenheim Memorial Foundation and Yale University for providing fellowships which allowed me to think and to map out this book. In the first years of my analytic training, I had the privilege of meeting weekly with Hans Loewald to discuss psychoanalytic theory and practice. In addition to the fact that I learned enormously from him, and had a chance to try out my ideas on a seasoned and sensitive analyst, our discussions helped me to think through how philosophy and psychoanalysis are related. I would also like to thank a number of people who read and criticized the manuscript in various stages: Rudiger Bittner, David Carlson, Wayne Downey, Christopher Dustin, Cynthia Farrar, Jonathan Galassi, Linda Healey, Hans Loewald, Linda Mayes, Ernst Prelinger, Mark Ravizza, Timothy Smiley, Al Solnit. Drafts of two chapters of this book were presented to the Muriel Gardiner Seminar in Psychoanalysis and the Humanities, and I am indebted to the participants for their comments. I have also taught a course at Yale, "Psychoanalysis and the Philosophy of Mind," in which the students' questions and reactions helped me to clarify my thinking on the central themes of this book. I am deeply indebted to my colleagues at the Western New England Institute for Psychoanalysis: they have provided an atmosphere which is supportive and challenging. Although Sophia Lear did not strictly speaking read the manuscript, I have learned as much from her about love and its role in individuation as from anyone.

BIBLIOGRAPHY

Aristotle. *The Complete Works of Aristotle: The Revised Oxford Translation*. Princeton: Princeton University Press, 1984.

Ayer, A. J. *Language, Truth and Logic*. Harmondsworth: Penguin, 1971.

Bettelheim, B. *Freud and Man's Soul*. New York: Knopf, 1983.

Blos, P. "The Genealogy of the Ego Ideal," *Psychoanalytic Study of the Child*, 29 (1974), pp. 95–103.

———. "The Contribution of Psychoanalysis to the Psychotherapy of Adolescents," *Psychoanalytic Study of the Child*, 38 (1983), pp. 577–600.

———. *On Adolescence*. Glencoe, Ill.: Free Press, 1962.

Brenner, C. "On the Nature and Development of Affects: A Unified Theory," *Psychoanalytic Quarterly*, XLIII (1974).

———. "Depression, Anxiety and Affect Theory," *International Journal of Psychoanalysis*, LV (1974).

———. "Affects and Psychic Conflict," *Psychoanalytic Quarterly*, XLIV (1975).

———. *The Mind in Conflict*. New York: International Universities Press, 1982.

Burge, T. "Individualism and the Mental," *Midwest Studies in Philosophy*, IV (1979).

Cavell, S. *Must We Mean What We Say?* Cambridge, Eng.: Cambridge University Press, 1976.

Chasseguet-Smirgel, J. *Creativity and Perversion*. New York: Norton, 1984.

———. *The Ego Ideal*. New York: Norton, 1985.

Clarke, T. "The Legacy of Skepticism," *Journal of Philosophy*, 1972.

Darwin, C. *The Expression of the Emotions in Man and Animals*. New York: Philosophical Library, 1955.

Davidson, D. *Essays on Actions and Events*. Oxford: Clarendon Press, 1980.

———. *Inquiries into Truth and Interpretation*. Oxford: Clarendon Press, 1984.

de Sousa, R. *The Rationality of Emotion*. Cambridge, Mass.: MIT Press, 1987.

Deutsch, F., ed. *On the Mysterious Leap from the Mind to the Body.* New York: International Universities Press, 1959.

Edelson, M. *Hypothesis and Evidence in Psychoanalysis.* Chicago: University of Chicago Press, 1984.

———. *Psychoanalysis: A Theory in Crisis.* Chicago: University of Chicago Press, 1988.

Ellenberger, H. *The Discovery of the Unconscious: The History and Evolution of Dynamic Psychiatry.* New York: Basic Books, 1970.

Fairbairn, W. R. D. *Psychoanalytic Studies of the Personality.* London: Routledge & Kegan Paul, 1984.

Farrar, C. *The Origins of Democratic Thinking: The Invention of Politics in Ancient Athens.* Cambridge, Eng.: Cambridge University Press, 1988.

Fenichel, O. *The Collected Papers of Otto Fenichel.* New York: David Lewis, 1927.

———. *Problems in Psychoanalytic Technique.* New York: Psychoanalytic Quarterly, 1941.

———. *The Psychoanalytic Theory of Neurosis.* New York: Norton, 1945.

Frankfurt, H. "Freedom of the Will and the Concept of a Person," *Journal of Philosophy,* 1971; reprinted in Gary Watson, ed., *Free Will* (Oxford: Oxford University Press, 1982), and in Harry Frankfurt, *The Importance of What We Care About* (Cambridge, Eng.: Cambridge University Press, 1988).

Freud, A. "Adolescence," *Psychoanalytic Study of the Child,* 13 (1958), pp. 255–78.

———. *The Ego and the Mechanisms of Defense.* New York: International Universities Press, 1985.

Freud, S. *The Standard Edition of the Complete Psychological Works of Sigmund Freud.* J. Strachey, trans. and ed., London: Hogarth Press, 1981.

———. *Gesammelte Werke, Chronologisch Geordnet.* A. Freud, E. Bibring et al., eds. London, 1940–52; Frankfurt am Main, 1968.

———. *The Complete Letters of Sigmund Freud to Wilhelm Fliess, 1887–1904.* J. M. Masson, trans. and ed. Cambridge, Mass.: Harvard University Press, 1985.

Freud, S. and Jung, C. G. *The Freud/Jung Letters: The Correspondence Between Sigmund Freud and C. G. Jung.* Princeton: Princeton University Press, 1974.

Gay, P. *Freud: A Life for Our Time.* New York: Norton, 1988.

Geuss, R. *The Idea of a Critical Theory: Habermas and the Frankfurt*

Bibliography · 227

School. Cambridge, Eng.: Cambridge University Press, 1981.
Glover, E. *The Technique of Psychoanalysis.* New York: International Universities Press, 1955.
Gordon, R. M. *The Structure of the Emotions.* Cambridge, Eng.: Cambridge University Press, 1987.
Greenberg, J. and S. Mitchell. *Object Relations in Psychoanalytic Theory.* Cambridge, Mass.: Harvard University Press, 1983.
Grice, H. P. "Meaning," in *Studies in the Way of Words.* Cambridge, Mass.: Harvard University Press, 1989.
Grunbaum, A. *The Foundations of Psychoanalysis.* Berkeley: University of California Press, 1984.
Habermas, J. *Knowledge and Human Interests.* London: Heinemann, 1978.
Hacker, P. *Insight and Illusion: Wittgenstein on Philosophy and the Metaphysics of Experience.* Oxford: Clarendon Press, 1972.
Hartmann, H. *Essays on Ego Psychology.* New York: International Universities Press, 1964.
Hegel, G. W. F. *Phenomenology of Spirit.* A. V. Miller, trans. New York: Oxford University Press, 1977.
———. *Philosophy of Right.* T. M. Knox, trans. New York: Oxford University Press, 1980.
———. *History of Philosophy.* E. S. Haldane and F. H. Simson, trans. New York: Humanities Press, 1974.
Jacobson, E. *The Self and the Object World.* New York: International Universities Press, 1964.
Kant, I. *Critique of Pure Reason.* New York: St. Martin's Press, 1965.
Kernberg, O. *Borderline Conditions and Pathological Narcissism.* New York: Aronson, 1975.
———. *Internal World and External Reality.* New York: Aronson, 1980.
———. *Severe Personality Disorders.* New Haven: Yale University Press, 1984.
Klein, M. *Love, Guilt and Reparation.* London: Hogarth Press, 1981.
———. *The Pyschoanalysis of Children.* London: Hogarth Press, 1980.
———. *Envy and Gratitude.* London: Hogarth Press, 1984.
Kneale, W. and M. *The Development of Logic.* Oxford: Clarendon Press, 1962.
Kohut, H. *The Analysis of the Self.* Madison, Conn.: International Universities Press, 1987.
———. *The Restoration of the Self.* Madison, Conn.: International Universities Press, 1986.

——. "The Two Analyses of Mr. Z," *International Journal of Psychoanalysis*, LX (1979).

Kuhn, T. *The Structure of Scientific Revolutions*. Chicago: University of Chicago Press, 1962.

Lacan, J. *Ecrits*. Paris: Editions du Seuil, 1966.

——. *Ecrits: A Selection*. A. Sheridan, trans. London: Tavistock, 1982.

Lampl DeGroot, J. "On Adolescence," *Psychoanalytic Study of the Child*, 15 (1960), pp. 95–103.

Laplanche, J. *Life and Death in Psychoanalysis*. Baltimore: Johns Hopkins, 1970.

Lear, J. "Leaving the World Alone," *Journal of Philosophy*, 1982.

——. "The Disappearing 'We,' " *Proceedings of the Aristotelian Society*, Supplementary Volume, 1984.

——. "Transcendental Anthropology," in P. Pettit and J. McDowell, eds., *Subject, Context and Thought*. Oxford: Clarendon Press, 1986.

——. *Aristotle: The Desire to Understand*. Cambridge, Eng.: Cambridge University Press, 1988.

——. "Katharsis," *Phronesis*, 1988.

Le Bon, G. *Psychologie des Foules*. Paris: F. Alcan, 1900.

——. *The Crowd: A Study of the Popular Mind*. New York: Penguin, 1977.

Lévy-Bruhl, L. *Les Fonctions Mentales dans les Sociétés Inférieures*. Paris: F. Alcan, 1910.

——. *How Natives Think*. L. A. Clare, trans. New York: Knopf, 1926.

Locke, J. *An Essay Concerning Human Understanding*. London: J. M. Dent, 1968.

Loewald, H. W. *Psychoanalysis and the History of the Individual*. New Haven: Yale University Press, 1978.

——. *Papers on Psychoanalysis*. New Haven: Yale University Press, 1980.

——. *Sublimation: Inquiries into Theoretical Psychoanalysis*. New Haven: Yale University Press, 1988.

Mackie, J. L. *Ethics: Inventing Right and Wrong*. New York: Penguin, 1977.

Mahler, M. *On Human Symbiosis and the Vicissitudes of Individuation*. I: *Infantile Psychosis*. New York: International Universities Press, 1967.

——. F. Pine and A. Bergman. *The Psychological Birth of the Human*

Infant: Symbiosis and Individuation. New York: Basic Books, 1975.

Mann, T. "Freud and the Future," in *Freud, Goethe, Wagner*. New York: Knopf, 1937. Originally published as *Freud und die Zukunft*. Vienna: Bermann-Fischer Verlag, 1936.

McDougall, J. *Plea for a Measure of Abnormality*. New York: International Universities Press, 1980.

Miller, A. *The Drama of the Gifted Child*. New York: Basic Books, 1981.

Mitchell, S. A. *Relational Concepts in Psychoanalysis*. Cambridge, Mass.: Harvard University Press, 1988.

Nagel, T. *Mortal Questions*. Cambridge, Eng.: Cambridge University Press, 1979.

Novey, S. "A Clinical View of Affect Theory in Psychoanalysis," *International Journal of Psychoanalysis*, XL (1959).

O'Shaughnessy, B. *The Will*. Cambridge, Eng.: Cambridge University Press, 1980.

———. "The Id and the Thinking Process," in R. Wollheim and J. Hopkins, eds., *Philosophical Essays on Freud*.

Person, E. *Dreams of Love and Fateful Encounters*. New York: Norton, 1988.

Plato. *Gorgias*. T. Irwin, trans. Oxford: Clarendon Press, 1979.

———. *Apology* (Socrates' Defense), in E. Hamilton and H. Cairns, eds., *The Collected Dialogues of Plato*. New York: Bollingen Foundation and Pantheon, 1964.

———. *Symposium*, in *The Collected Dialogues of Plato*.

Popper, K. R. *The Open Society and Its Enemies*. Princeton: Princeton University Press, 1966.

Proust, M. *A la Recherche du Temps Perdu*. Paris: Gallimard, 1987.

———. *Remembrance of Things Past*. C. K. Scott Moncrieff and T. Kilmartin, trans. New York: Random House, 1981.

Pulver, S. "Can Affects Be Unconscious?" *International Journal of Psychoanalysis*, LII (1971).

Quine, W. V. O. "Carnap and Logical Truth," in *The Ways of Paradox*. New York: Random House, 1966.

———. "Two Dogmas of Empiricism," in *From a Logical Point of View*. New York: Harper & Row, 1963.

———. *Word and Object*. Cambridge, Mass.: MIT Press, 1970.

Rappaport, D. "On the Psychoanalytical Theory of Affects," *International Journal of Psychoanalysis*, XXXIV (1953).

————. *The Structure of Psychoanalytic Theory: A Systematizing Attempt,* Psychological Issues 2, monograph 6, 1960.

Ricouer, P. *Freud and Philosophy.* New Haven: Yale University Press, 1970.

Ritvo, S. "Late Adolescence: Developmental and Clinical Considerations," *Psychoanalytic Study of the Child,* 26 (1971), pp. 253–57.

Roberts, R. C. "What an Emotion Is: A Sketch," *Philosophical Review,* XLVII (1988).

Sachs, D. "In Fairness to Freud," *Philosophical Review,* XLVIII (1989).

Schafer, R. "The Clinical Analysis of Affects," *Journal of the American Psychoanalytic Association,* XII (1964).

————. *Aspects of Internalization.* New York: International Universities Press, 1968.

————. *A New Language for Psychoanalysis.* New Haven: Yale University Press, 1976.

————. *The Analytic Attitude.* New York: Basic Books, 1983.

Schur, M. "Affects and Cognition," *International Journal of Psychoanalysis,* L (1969).

Shope, R. "Freud's Concepts of Meaning," *Psychoanalysis and Contemporary Science,* II (1973).

Spence, D. *Narrative Truth and Historical Truth: Meaning and Interpretation in Psychoanalysis.* New York: Norton, 1982.

Spitz, R. A. "Genesis of Psychiatric Conditions in Early Childhood (Hospitalism)," *Psychoanalytic Study of the Child,* 1 (1945), pp. 53–74.

————. "Hospitalism: A Follow-up Study," *Psychoanalytic Study of the Child,* 2 (1946), pp. 113–17.

Stalnaker, R. *Inquiry.* Cambridge, Mass.: MIT Press, 1984.

Stern, D. *The Interpersonal World of the Infant.* New York: Basic Books, 1985.

Sullivan, H. S. *The Interpersonal Theory of Psychiatry.* New York: Norton, 1953.

————. *Clinical Studies in Psychiatry.* New York: Norton, 1956.

Sulloway, F. *Freud: Biologist of the Mind.* New York: Basic Books, 1979.

Taylor, C. "Responsibility for Self," in G. Watson, ed., *Free Will.* Oxford: Oxford University Press, 1982.

————. "Self-Interpreting Animals," in *Human Agency and Language: Philosophical Papers,* I. Cambridge, Eng.: Cambridge University Press, 1985.

Thucydides. *History of the Peloponnesian War*. R. Crawley, trans. New York: Random House, 1934.

Velleman, D. *Practical Reflection*. Princeton: Princeton University Press, 1989.

Watson, G. "Free Agency," in G. Watson, ed., *Free Will*. Oxford: Oxford University Press, 1982.

Williams, B. *Descartes: The Project of Pure Enquiry*. New York: Penguin, 1978.

———. *Shame and Necessity*. Berkeley: University of California Press, in press.

Winnicott, D. W. *The Maturational Process and the Facilitating Environment*. London: Hogarth Press, 1982.

———. *The Child, the Family and the Outside World*. New York: Penguin, 1984.

———. *Through Paediatrics to Psycho-Analysis*. London: Hogarth Press, 1975.

Wittgenstein, L. *Tractatus Logico-Philosophicus*. D. F. Pears and B. F. McGuinness, trans. London: Routledge & Kegan Paul, 1974.

———. *Philosophical Investigations*. Oxford: Basil Blackwell, 1958.

Wolf, S. "Sanity and the Metaphysics of Responsibility," in F. Schoeman, ed., *Responsibility, Character and the Emotions*. Cambridge, Eng.: Cambridge University Press, 1987.

Wollheim, R. *Sigmund Freud*. Cambridge, Eng.: Cambridge University Press, 1981.

———. *The Thread of Life*. Cambridge, Eng.: Cambridge University Press, 1984.

———. "The Mind and the Mind's Image of Itself," in *On Art and the Mind*. Cambridge, Mass.: Harvard University Press, 1974.

——— and J. Hopkins, eds. *Philosophical Essays on Freud*. Cambridge, Eng.: Cambridge University Press, 1982.

INDEX